THE COYOTE CYCLE

THE COYOTE CYCLE

SEVEN PLAYS BY

MURRAY MEDNICK

CONTENTS

I: POINTING

"Woodchucks fuckin' in the trees." Darrell
Larson as COYOTE in *Pointing*.

TRICKSTER (Norbert Weisser) explodes
from the earth on his entrance in *Pointing*.

THE SCENE: A clearing in the woods at dusk. It is quiet for awhile, then COYOTE falls from the tree cover above. He is wearing a black leather jacket, a tee-shirt with the figure of a hand on it, jeans, sneakers; carries a silver arrow on his back, assorted "weapons" and an inflated bear-bladder on his hip. He announces:

COYOTE: Coyote was sent by Earthmaker on a mission, which is to destroy the evil spirits afflicting mankind! *(Pauses, makes a spiraling movement)* To make the waterfall come to Earth. *(Pause)* He bounced around, doing the best he could. Most of the time he forgot. He made a lot of dumb mistakes. He's not good, and he's not bad — but he's tricky. *(Stops, listens; with an obeisant gesture to the sky)* You have to climb high into the mountains, way above the snow line! *(Seems to hear something, freezes; listens hard, points.)* THERE! *(Drops the point, but remains extremely alert, as HARE.)* Coyote is an Outlaw, a Wanted Man... *(Forgets HARE and points with formidable power in the other three directions.)* THERE! THERE! THERE!

(TRICKSTER explodes out of the ground with a mournful cry. He is dressed neatly in a suit but is mud-encrusted and bone-weary. COYOTE circles him in amazement.)

COYOTE: Are you a human being?

TRICKSTER: *(As though blinded)* Is my body attached? Is my body attached? Is my body...? Can you see it?

COYOTE: A muddy man! A mental man!

TRICKSTER: *(Opening his eyes)* I was in a place where the beings had only heads! I had to go deep into the earth to get my body back! Deep down into the ground. And keep my eyes closed and not look around! I had to get my body back!

COYOTE: What did you see down there?

TRICKSTER: I kept my eyes closed.

COYOTE: Right! Did you feel anything?

TRICKSTER: Going down, I didn't have no body. Coming back, I grew bones and meat stuck to them. My skin tightened on the heart. I could feel the nerves, taste the blood, sense the pulse. *(Stops, convulses)* I have my body! *(Rhythmically jerks and stomps.)*

COYOTE: *(Referring to the ground)* Don't scratch it!

TRICKSTER: I have my body!

COYOTE: Don't scratch it! Leave it alone!

TRICKSTER: My bones rattle when I dance! My bones rattle when I dance! My heart has a skin! I —

COYOTE: *(Pointing)* There! *(TRICKSTER , shocked out of his dance, assumes his protective posture and grunts; COYOTE struts; TRICK-STER looks up into the tree with some bemusement.)*

TRICKSTER: Did you break any bones?

COYOTE: No.

TRICKSTER: That was quite an interesting fall.

COYOTE: You could see that?

TRICKSTER: I could hear it. It was like the thunder.

COYOTE: It was from another world! Way above the snow line! Coyote returns from the upper world by sliding down the spider web!

TRICKSTER: *(Looking up at the net in the tree.)* Is that what that is, a spider web?

COYOTE: No. It's twine netting.

TRICKSTER: *(Recovering)* This is a nice spot. I'm glad I came up here.

COYOTE: It's right along the trail. People ride by on melancholy horses. *(Musing)* Melancholy horses....

TRICKSTER: What did you see up there?

COYOTE: *(Pretending)* Where?

TRICKSTER: In the upper world.

COYOTE: Woodchucks fuckin' in the trees.

TRICKSTER: Outasight. Woodchucks fuckin' in the trees. Outasight.

COYOTE: Yeah. *(Pause)* Where'd you come from? Originally, I mean.

TRICKSTER: *(Pointing)* THERE! *(COYOTE is startled but takes his protective posture. TRICKSTER smiles, dropping the point; looks up into the tree.)* That was some fall. My father fell out of a tree when he was a kid. Hasn't been the same since. At least, that's the story. I — *(COYOTE points)*

COYOTE: There! I feel strong! I feel strong enough to go on the warpath!

TRICKSTER: *(Recovering)* Who are you mad at?

COYOTE: You don't have to be mad to go on the warpath. You just go on the warpath. You don't need to make any excuses.

TRICKSTER: *(Offering his hand)* My name's Smith.

COYOTE: Brown. What's your personal history? Tell me about yourself.

TRICKSTER: I have no personal history. I've given it up.

COYOTE: You got any spare change? *(TRICKSTER rummages, produces coins.)* Thank you. What do you do for a living?

TRICKSTER: I hunt. I stalk. I track people down.

COYOTE: You hunt people?

TRICKSTER: I always get my man.

(COYOTE makes a big show of berating and destroying one of his weapons.)

COYOTE: WHAT ARE YOU DOING? YOU ARE A USELESS
BURDEN! I AM TIRED OF CARRYING YOU AROUND ALL THE
TIME! TAKE A HIKE! Etc. *(Throws the broken weapon away. To
TRICKSTER:)* You'll never get Coyote! *(Crosses to TRICKSTER'S
hole.)* Tell me what's down there.

TRICKSTER: Where?

COYOTE: *(Pointing down into the hole)* In the lower world.

TRICKSTER: It's kinda sandy. Hot. *(He moves away, avoiding the hole.)*
I don't know. My eyes were closed... *(He is snapped about as if by a
force in the hole.)* Hot! Savage hatred! Anger! Vengefulness!
Helpless... *(Pulled by his navel toward the hole)* I saw tracks. Man
tracks. I was coming from a place where the beings had only heads.
A voice said: "See, foot markings. Not the bear, not the wolf. Where
have they come from? Where are they going? See if you can
follow." I put my face in the dust and closed my eyes. I felt
unarmed. I was vulnerable. I thought, "Who is this man? Where
is he leading me?" But I followed the tracks. I am a hunter. I was
compelled. It was my fate. *(Falls to his knees above the hole)* I went
down, down. I came to a lake. There, on the other side of the lake,
was the man, standing on a buffalo head, pointing at me! The
buffalo head was shining white, white as the salt flat, hot white! The
man was pointing at me! I looked up: it was the roof of a cave, sky-
blue! "DON'T KILL ME!" the man shouted...!

COYOTE: *(Pointing)* There! *(TRICKSTER leaps to his feet, taking his
protective posture.)* When Coyote goes on the warpath, he goes
alone! *(Makes a big commotion while destroying another weapon.)* Here
's another one! He's very sensitive! He's very emotional! He's
insulted! I'm tired of it! Take a hike! Etc.

TRICKSTER: I don't see how anybody can go on the warpath and be
as dumb as you are.

COYOTE: I don't need it. It's just clutter. Useless clutter. That stuff
just gets in the way, drags me down. I don't need no weapons!
When you go on the warpath, you go on the warpath! It's clean!
(Waves a hand at TRICKSTER, who takes a step back and sizes him up.)

TRICKSTER: Can you do anything well?

COYOTE: I know plants. I'm a master of plant life. *(Blurting)* I got things planted around here.

TRICKSTER: *(Sly)* What kind of things?

COYOTE: *(Offhand)* Things to remind me. Mementoes. Plants are voices, messengers to Coyote. They tell him where he is, which way he's going, what's behind him. *(Finds a solitary cactus)* This plant here calls to me. He has something to say to me. *(Assumes a listening posture)* Yes, little brother?

(TRICKSTER finds a stump or rock to sit on upstage and becomes the "voice" of the plant.)

TRICKSTER: Don't listen to me, Coyote. My tale is a sad one, a story that kills.

COYOTE: Coyote always wakes up again.

TRICKSTER: It is killing to the spirit.

COYOTE: The spirit of Coyote is as unquenchable as the waterfall! He is not afraid! *(For a moment TRICKSTER becomes OWL, causing COYOTE to become a frightened HARE.)*

TRICKSTER: The Owl never sleeps.

COYOTE: Is that your animal? The Owl?

TRICKSTER: When the Owl is heard, someone dies.

COYOTE: Coyote can't die!

TRICKSTER: I'll tell you a thing or two, but try not to listen.

COYOTE: Coyote can eat it!

TRICKSTER: My nature is sorrowful. My great Mother weeps, and no one hears. The stars see her distress, but they cannot help her. They are too far away. My Mother's hair is torn from her head by the roots. She has steeped her eyes in burning ashes. Her body is swollen, her blood has turned sour. Sharp edges are in her genitals, her breasts bleed, her womb is collapsed.

COYOTE: What have they done!

TRICKSTER: The Sun takes pity on her, the Moon wobbles in its grief. My Mother's anger is a terrible thing! She longs to tremble, she longs to defecate, she wishes to vomit! She wants to purify herself. But out of compassion, she refrains. Out of charity, she remains still. Out of love, she accomodates herself.

COYOTE: *(Going berserk)* Those assholes! They've pissed on my mother! They've shit in her face! They've poured acid into her liver! They've dumped garbage into her stomach! They've poured filth into her veins, dust into her lungs, disease into the marrow of her bones! Those assholes! Treacherous maniacs! Rip-off artists! Hustlers! Ingrates! Stinking animals! Insensitive beasts! Blind! Selfish! Ferocious dogs! Stupid! Slavish! Ugly, heartless assholes! I'll destroy them all!

TRICKSTER: *(Pointing)* There!

COYOTE: My God! I've fallen into my own shit! I didn't mean that! *(Walks away. TRICKSTER approaches the Audience.)*

TRICKSTER: I'm a traveling man. I'm a hunter, a stalker, a spy. I've seen that there's no escape. We're in the soup. My stomach is full of bad songs. *(Starts away, then turns suddenly with the aspect of an angry old man)* Revenge! Revenge for the torture! Revenge on the grabbers! Revenge on the know-it-alls! The smug! Those smegma heads! *(COYOTE rushes downstage to re-capture the Audience's attention.)*

COYOTE: I'll tell a Coyote tale!

TRICKSTER: *(Menacing)* Watch out for the Owl, Coyote! Watch out for the Crow! *(Flaps his wings, caws, and retires upstage. COYOTE ignores him.)*

COYOTE: One morning Coyote woke up and his blanket was gone. Then he looked into the sky and he saw a banner in the sky. He said, "Oh boy, must be feast day! They only fly a banner when it's feast day!" So he jumped to his feet. And it was then he realized that it wasn't a banner at all: it was his blanket on the end of his penis! So he said to his penis, "Little brother, if you keep this up we'll lose the blanket!" And he rolled his penis up and put it in a box on his back and he folded up his blanket and he went along. And he came to the shore of a lake. And there on the other side of the lake were *women...* swimming! And one of the women was the Chief's daughter. Coyote said, "Now is the opportune time. I will have intercourse!" So he sent his penis across the lake, but as it went it hit the top of the water and made waves! So he reeled it back it in, and he said, "No, no little brother! If you do it like that, you will scare them!" And he took a fine rock and he put the rock on the end of his penis and he sent the penis across the lake. But the rock was too heavy, and his penis hit the bottom of the lake! So, he brought the penis back again and he took that rock off and put another rock on and this rock was just right. And he sent his penis across the lake and it went so fast that it hit some of the women and upset them. So they swam for the shore, but the Chief's daughter was too slow and the penis went right in her! Now all the women were frightened and ran to get the men! Who are strong! But they couldn't get the penis out! They had to find the Old Woman who knew what to do in matters of this kind. And she came and recognized Coyote right away. She yelled across the lake, "First-born, come out of there!" But of course, he wouldn't! They had to hire a Chipmunk to come and take care of it. The Chipmunk went right in there and chewed the penis into little pieces. And Coyote came across the lake and he gathered up all the pieces and he went running through the forest throwing the pieces around and wherever they landed was food! One piece was potato and one piece was artichoke and one piece was sharp-claw berry and one piece was rice... And that is why our penis is shaped the way it is!

TRICKSTER: *(Dryly)* Where were you in '68? *(He musically supports COYOTE'S ensuing riff by joining him on the phrases in caps.)*

COYOTE: Traveling. I was sitting by the waterfall trying to describe the waterfall it was the most lovely waterfall trying to get a grip on things describe the waterfall in my notebook on the bridge only goddamn it I have lost my right hand I HAVE LOST MY RIGHT HAND trying to describe the waterfall as it goes MY RIGHT HAND in the current my head sucking air UP UP How did I get into the water I was sitting on the bridge with my notebook in my LEFT hand as it goes into the water cool and strong flows past WHERE IS MY RIGHT HAND courses through me I mean actually courses through me THE ROCKS watch out for the rocks goddamn it But I have got my head up I have got my head up Watch out for the rocks MY RIGHT HAND the water is COLD it has got COLD under the bridge deep green cold fast nobody knows where it goes how deep goddamn it MY RIGHT HAND Has God got my RIGHT HAND Has God got my right hand Who is God that he should have my right hand when I am alone in the river Give me my right hand back God there is no God there is no right hand but I need my right hand my LEFT hand is busy keeping me in the water How did I get into the water How could I go into the water without my right hand trying to describe the waterfall the SPEED of it no that is not true that is not an accurate description of the waterfall see the waterfall has no TIME in it the waterfall has no TIME in it and I must be STILL therefore I must be still If I am still I will get my right hand back No no that is not the reason I must be still my LEFT hand is busy too busy to describe the waterfall trying to get a grip on a ROCK grab onto a ROCK if I am still I will SINK no no that is not the reason The water is moving me I am being moved in the water that is not true either There is no MOTION in the water There is no MOTION in the water That would not be an accurate description of the waterfall to say something about the waterfall with my RIGHT HAND while the LEFT hand is keeping me up in the water busy keeping me up in the water then the RIGHT HAND–

(He stops, staring at his right hand. TRICKSTER points.)

TRICKSTER: There! *(COYOTE takes his protective posture.)*

COYOTE: I heard that! I have heard myself! Why have I done this? I have made myself suffer! *(To Audience)* I know–Coyote's RIGHT hand fought his LEFT hand for the buffalo meat... *(He retires, pondering, as TRICKSTER approaches the Audience.)*

TRICKSTER: Here's a Trickster story! A long, long time ago, way before people painted their lives onto cave walls, Earthmaker had made earth "just so." People had nothing to worry about. Earthmaker took care of everything. In the morning you opened your window and there was breakfast, already made. In the afternoon, there was lunch, and in the evening, dinner. Everything was "just so." There was no pain, no suffering. Everyone smiled and was happy. Everyone, that is, except Coyote/Trickster. He was BORED. He walked around with a sour face all the time. One day, when he couldn't stand it anymore, he stopped everything and everybody and screamed, "Why are you so happy? Why do you walk around with those bovine, stupid grins on your faces? What is there to smile about? Nothing, NOTHING is happening!" "What do you mean nothing is happening?," the people said, "Nothing needs to happen. Everything is JUST SO." Coyote/Trickster looked up at Earthmaker and howled, "Ahhooooo." "What would you like to happen?" the people asked him. He paused, thought a little, and then answered: "I know. What we need here is Death." "Death? What do you mean, Death?" the people said. "I mean Death. The end. Over and out. You put a limit on life and perhaps you assholes start paying some attention to living. Put some meaning into the middle. Stop that stupid grinning." People shrugged their shoulders and went on with their lives, happily smiling as always and soon they'd forgotten the whole thing. Except for Earthmaker who never forgets. A few days or years later, there was a footrace and everyone was in it, including Coyote/Trickster's oldest son, who was one of the fastest runners. And he was running and running and passing people and he was just about to win when BAMM he stepped on a rattlesnake and keeled over and stopped breathing. This had never happened before, so people told him to get up and run. But he wouldn't. So they called Coyote/Trickster and he came and shook him and shook him and said, "Wake up oldest son of mine. This is no time to sleep. This is a time to run and win and bring honor to your family." But he wouldn't wake up or start breathing. It was then that Coyote/Trickster remembered his outburst from before. So he looked up at Earthmaker and shouted, "Earthmaker, what I said a while back was a joke! I didn't mean a word I said! I was joking! So you just wake my oldest son up and make him breathe again! That way he can win the race and bring honor to his family and we forget the whole thing! What do you say, Earthmaker?... Earthmaker? *(Long Silence. TRICKSTER howls. Pause.)* And since that time there has been Death on Earth.

(COYOTE rushes over to show the bag he's been wearing.)

COYOTE: Hoho! You know what this is?

TRICKSTER: No, what is it?

COYOTE: It's a bear bladder. Can you imagine that? When the bear takes a leak, he takes a leak! The bear can out-piss the Coyote any day of the week!

TRICKSTER: What you got in there? You carrying bear piss around with you in there?

COYOTE: You wanna look inside?

TRICKSTER: No.

COYOTE: What I have in here is tiny little children.

TRICKSTER: Oh?

COYOTE: Right.

TRICKSTER: Who are they?

COYOTE: The sons and daughters of my brothers and sisters. My brother the Silver Fox, my sister the Chipmunk, my sister the Antelope, my nephew the White Buffalo, my brother the Sphinx, my —

TRICKSTER: How many of them are there?

COYOTE: A couple hundred...

TRICKSTER: What are you doing with them?

COYOTE: If I ever get stuck somewhere with no food, I can eat them.

TRICKSTER: Wily of you.

COYOTE: Right.

TRICKSTER: Show me one.

(COYOTE reaches into the bladder and produces an invisible child.)

COYOTE: You can't see them. They're quite small, and they're not made of flesh, they're made of power. *(TRICKSTER reacts.)* I suppose you can hardly wait to taste one. *(COYOTE puts the child back into the bladder.)* Well, you can't have any.

TRICKSTER: Why not?

COYOTE: Your stomach is full of bad songs... *(Wanders away... to himself)* Yesterday I saw smoke... Outside Alamagordo... I had to lead a whole bunch of people back through a hole in the sky... *(Jerks and trembles like a dog)* I have to lie down and rest now.

(COYOTE lies down, cradling the bladder, places his silver arrow so that it points out from his anus. He closes his eyes and appears to be asleep. TRICKSTER observes him and then advances.)

COYOTE: *(Continuing)* Stay back! This spot is guarded. We've got you covered! My little brother, the asshole is on the case! He is the toughest cop this side of the Rocky Mountains! One false move and you're in the shit! *(TRICKSTER stops in his tracks. Considers.)*

TRICKSTER: You know, Coyote, I'm hip to where your honey spots are.

COYOTE: Honey spots?

TRICKSTER: You know what I'm talkin' about. I know where each of them spots is.

COYOTE: No you don't. Your sense of smell is dead. Your sense of place is dead. You can't tell one spot from another.

(While COYOTE suffers, TRICKSTER digs up, one by one, a series of five small figurines buried in the ground, each revelation accompanied by a specific, appropriate, gesture and sound.)

TRICKSTER: They don't call me Trickster for nothing. See, I watched where you buried your goods. *(Tears come to COYOTE'S eyes.)* I am a bounty hunter. I work on a piece basis. And I always get my man.

(COYOTE jumps to his feet and angrily breaks his arrow.)

COYOTE: Useless! Useless suffering!

(TRICKSTER approaches him holding the figurines.)

TRICKSTER: These are your honey spots. These are the moments of your buried love. Here are the moments of passion, of sweet affection, of tenderness. Here is the blood, the pulse, the nerves of the body, the sex. Here are the deep feelings — joy and pain. The face of the beloved, the voice of the beloved, the beloved as she comes to you, as she opens her arms to you. The kiss of the beloved. Here is your grief at separation. Here also is your fear, your jealousy, your greed to possess.

COYOTE: You thief! You voyeur! You lousy spy! Why don't we stop fucking around and prepare for battle? Coyote and Trickster, one on one!

TRICKSTER: I don't want to fight, I want to eat. I've become a human being. I'm a person now, and I have to learn how to eat.

COYOTE: Can you eat the food that is prepared for you, Trickster? Look what you have in your hands already. Can you eat? Do you have the stomach? Can you bear it? This is powerful food you got there in your hands, very special stuff, stuff of the spirit.

(TRICKSTER cautiously sniffs, then touches the dolls with his lips.)

TRICKSTER: They're made of straw.

COYOTE: You must know how to eat them. Are you a human being?

(TRICKSTER licks them, tries to take a bite.)

COYOTE: Hoho! You want to know what those things are? You know what those are? Ha! When the chipmunk bit off my penis, he buried the pieces here on this spot! You've just been eating my dick! Hoho!

(TRICKSTER flings the figurines away.)

TRICKSTER: To death, Coyote!

COYOTE: Coyote cannot die!

(TRICKSTER becomes CROW. COYOTE points when the CROW loses

power. COYOTE finds a spot and becomes BLUE JAY. TRICKSTER points when the BLUE JAY falters.)

TRICKSTER: I'll bring it into your feet! Into the groin! The bowels! The lungs! The head! I'll stalk you to death!

COYOTE: Coyote is immortal! His home is in the upper world, while Trickster wanders forever in the earth!

(TRICKSTER finds a spot and becomes OWL. COYOTE points when the OWL wavers.)

TRICKSTER: No! Not forever!

COYOTE: Forever, Trickster! As long as Earth lives, Trickster lives!

(COYOTE becomes COYOTE. TRICKSTER points. The battle is over. COYOTE takes his posture which he holds until his final speech.)

TRICKSTER: No! I want to get out of my body! I want to go back to the place where the beings have only heads! I don't want to be flesh. I want to be a clean white bone sticking out of the ground! I want to be a line! I want to be a sign, a scrawl, a circle on a rock! I want to be a rock!

COYOTE: You have to get way above the snow line... on the mountain peak. In the sky. Way above the snow line...

(TRICKSTER is trying to crawl back into the earth.)

TRICKSTER: I want to go down! I want to go down into the earth! Into the ground! Down into the center of the earth!

(COYOTE gently retrains him in the darkening twilight.)

COYOTE: No Trickster. Stay. It's all right. Listen. It's quiet. Look, all around us it is beautiful. Look, we're here — in the middle. *(Gestures.)* The waterfall comes to earth. It's all right.

(He makes the spiraling movement... Then they disappear– COYOTE back up the tree, TRICKSTER into the earth.)

END

Norbert Weisser as TRICKSTER in *Pointing*.

II: The Shadow Ripens

THE SCENE: Night. The remains of an ancient adobe dwelling on the side of a hill. Downstage center, a can of sterno burns in an old ceramic pot. Upstage, right, SPIDER WOMAN sits on a throne made of tree stumps and rocks. Her attitude is one of majestic repose. Behind her, extending into the distance, are the dimly lit outlines of many skulls, bones, and black and white banners, like Tibetan prayer flags, fluttering in the wind — this is "The Land of the Dead." Down right of SPIDER WOMAN stands the CLOWN in a small clearing of her own. Her posture is frozen, as though overwhelmed by a new, fearful responsibility. To the right of the Clown, attached by a line to SPIDER WOMAN's throne, is another rope web in the trees and brush.

Once the Audience is settled, there is a long wait as CLOWN slowly rotates her eyes to look at them. Shocked, she slowly rotates her body to alignment with her eyes. She is paralyzed there, bent over with indecision—which way to run? Suddenly, she breaks across to downstage left and is stopped there. Nowhere to run. She turns to face the Audience. Mute, CLOWN talks only with her hands (in Standard American Sign Language), and SPIDER WOMAN translates most of what she says.

SPIDER WOMAN: So. What's your story, kid?

CLOWN: *(Signing)* I can't talk!

SPIDER WOMAN: I know you can't talk. But can you listen?

CLOWN: *(Signing)* Yes! I got good ears!

SPIDER WOMAN: You got good ears, eh? *(Indicating CLOWN's progress)* What happened? *(CLOWN signs.)* You felt that when you moved your eyes, the air was disturbed? *(CLOWN nods vigorously.)* I see.

CLOWN: *(Signing)* I came into this life a human being, with parents!

SPIDER WOMAN: You came into this life a human being, with parents. Good for you.

CLOWN: *(Signing)* It's not good and it's not bad!

SPIDER WOMAN: Oh, it's not good and it's not bad.

CLOWN: *(Signing)* I got-got scared! I didn't know if I could do it! My parents expected me to do it!

SPIDER WOMAN: You got scared. You didn't know if you could do it. You're parents expected you to do it. *(Pause)* Do what?

CLOWN: *(Signing)* Be a human being!

SPIDER WOMAN: Be a human being. Well, that's a hard thing. Even Mr. Coyote might have to do that, when the time comes.

CLOWN: *(Making a face)* Coyote!

SPIDER WOMAN: Coyote.

CLOWN: *(Signing)* They expected me to get-get married! And have children! And make money!

SPIDER WOMAN: They expected you to get married, and have children, and make money! *(Pause)* And?

CLOWN: *(Signing)* I hit the road. I ate many powerful substances and took-took a lot of abuse from people. Now I can't talk no more.

SPIDER WOMAN: You hit the road. You took many powerful substances and took a lot of abuse from people, and now you can't talk... Someday you'll talk.

CLOWN: *(Signing)* I can't talk.

SPIDER WOMAN: You'll talk.

CLOWN: *(Signing)* I love Trickster. Don't tell him.

SPIDER WOMAN: *(Laughing)* You love Trickster! I won't tell him. What about Coyote?

CLOWN: *(Signing)* He's funny-weird!

SPIDER WOMAN: You're a little strange yourself.

CLOWN: *(Signing)* I am!

SPIDER WOMAN: You are what?

CLOWN: *(Signing)* Strange. Clown-strange. You teach me! You teach me to be divine! Clown-divine!

SPIDER WOMAN: Clown-divine... All right. I'll teach you.

CLOWN: *(Signing)* I'll work. You teach me!

SPIDER WOMAN: I'll teach you. *(CLOWN races happily back to her original spot.)* But don't interfere. One thing you have to learn is your place. Don't do anything unless you get a signal from me!

CLOWN: *(Signing)* Okay! But what do I do first?

SPIDER WOMAN: *(Reaching behind her for a Tibetan bell.)* First you get ready to hit this bell. When I say "LEFT HAND", you hit the bell.

CLOWN: *(Shows "Left Hand.")*

SPIDER WOMAN: Left hand. Right. *(CLOWN shows "Right Hand.")* Left hand! *(CLOWN switches hands. SPIDER WOMAN nods approval.)* Now you ought to know a little bit about how the world got made. *(Prepares to take the SPIDER WOMAN Posture, centerstage.)*

CLOWN: *(Signing)* What do I do after I hit the bell?

SPIDER WOMAN: *(Annoyed)* I don't know what happens after you hit the bell. We'll have to play it by ear.

CLOWN: *(Shows "Ear.")*

SPIDER WOMAN: *(Taking the Posture)* First, they say, there was only the Creator, Taiowa. So Taiowa created Sotuknang, in order to make things manifest, and to help carry out the harmonious plan of Creation. *(Proudly)* Sotuknang went to the universe, which was to be the First World, and out of it — he created ME, Spider Woman. When I awoke to life and received my name, I asked, "Why am I here?" "Look about you," said Sotuknang, "Here is this earth we have created, but there is no life on it. We see no joyful movement, we hear no joyful sound. What is life without sound and movement?" So I took some earth. *(She scoops up a handful. Spits into it.)*

And I molded the earth into two beings, twins. And one was Sound and one was Movement. Naturally, the two little critters sat right up and asked, "Who are we? And why are we here?" *(To her right hand)* You are here to help keep this world in order! *(To her left hand)* And you are here to send out sound! *(Indicates her left hand to CLOWN)* What are you waiting for? Hit the bell!

CLOWN: *(Signing)* You didn't say, "left hand"!

SPIDER WOMAN: I showed left hand! *(Demonstrates)* LEFT HAND! *(CLOWN hits the bell. COYOTE, wearing bells on his ankles, is seen and heard way off running towards us.)* And all the vibratory centers along the earth's axis from pole to pole resounded to the call! The whole earth trembled! The universe quivered in tune! Thus the whole world was made an instrument of sound, resounding praise to the Creator of all! *(She looks off.)* Here comes Coyote, running! *(She makes the posture and gesture indicating: "Fooling around with the gravity.")* Ha! Coyote is known as Imitator, because he only does what other people do! *(Scoffing, she returns to her throne. COYOTE arrives and stops short, declaring:)*

COYOTE: Coyote can run a thousand miles and never get tired! He is never even out of breath! Coyote can fly over the land in leaps and bounds! *(He tries to catch his breath.)* Wait a minute! This is a funny place! Someone has been fooling around with the gravity here! I don't like it! *(He breathes fast, resisting the pull of gravity. SPIDER WOMAN breathes with him.)* This place is like under water! *(He shouts, defiantly)* Coyote is great! He has attained life by his own powers! *(SPIDER WOMAN scoffs.)* I know what I'll do! I'll go fishing! *(Winking at the Audience, but still struggling with the pull of gravity, he points to a spot and seems to be fishing there.)* I'm an excellent fisherman! Actually, I do everything well — it's a gift from Taiowa! Coyote always catches something!

SPIDER WOMAN: *(Breathing intensely)* The shadow is ripening! The shadow ripens!

(An old Buffalo head-bone appears out of the ground behind COYOTE.)

COYOTE: I know you're down there, hiding under a rock! You'll make a fine dinner for Coyote!

SPIDER WOMAN: The shadow is ripening! *(TRICKSTER'S head appears under the buffalo head-bone— he has aged into an old man.)* The shadow ripens! *(TRICKSTER squirms partly out of the ground. COYOTE spins about to face it.)*

TRICKSTER: Coyote! Help me out of here!

COYOTE: Hoho! I knew you were coming up over there! I was only pretending over here!

TRICKSTER: Hey, what is this? What's going on here? I think the gravity is bad in this place! I'm having a very hard time of it! Even my bones are too heavy!

COYOTE: Well, what are you doing down there? Nobody told you to go down there.

TRICKSTER: I was sent on a very important mission by Spider Woman! Only a great warrior could accomplish such a mission! Do you think I was having fun down there? Look, it has turned my hair white! It was a very hard job!

COYOTE: *(As if under water)* Tell me about it!

TRICKSTER: Coyote, I don't like the sound of things here. The sound has weight. *(Pause)* Things are very thick here.

COYOTE: No doubt you have heard of me, Old Man. I am Coyote!

TRICKSTER: Who? *(Subsides into a trance)*

SPIDER WOMAN: Trickster!

TRICKSTER: *(Aroused)* There is a tribe! They live on a polar ice cap. Things were very clean there for a long time. And then something happened. It got all fucked up. A plague hit that tribe. There were accidents and tragedies and people were sad and they couldn't understand it. They called Spider Woman, and she called me! She knew I was the very man for the job!

COYOTE: Well, get to the main part. We don't have all night.

TRICKSTER: I had to sit on top of a hill by myself. I had to sing in harmony from that hill. Hey, it's not far from this place here.

COYOTE: I know that hill! I leave my scent there! That's one of MY places!

TRICKSTER: Well, I got to join that tribe on the polar ice cap! I knew I had to swim down though the bedrock. Heh, heh, I've been that way before.

COYOTE: You don't look well, Old Man. Have a Lucky Strike, it'll bring you luck. (TRICKSTER breaks the cigarette and throws it at him.) And if you need anything else, let me know.

SPIDER WOMAN: Trickster!

COYOTE: I'll try to do something for you — so long as it doesn't cost me any money.

TRICKSTER: An igloo was built! Seal skins covered the walls and the floors. I sat on a high stage. We all got our centers vibrating. We spoke in a language never heard before, and I began!

COYOTE: Let me talk now! I don't know about you, but I have had a great time myself! I have gone running! I ran all around this earth! I saw the holy mountain at the head-bone of the earth! It was next to a magical blue lake. You could look into that lake and see wonderful things — things of the future, things of the past, things of the upper world.

(SPIDER WOMAN intensifies the gravity.)

TRICKSTER: I think they gave me drugs, those strange people! I thought I was going to die! I was afraid to die! The gravity had changed! The center had changed! I felt fever! I felt trembling! I was falling! My blood stream was poisoned! The blood was pumping! I heard overwhelming sounds, like earthquake, like thunder!

COYOTE: I saw people who were beasts of burden. I saw them from my high place, where I sing my song. All around me they were building, building. They were making it tough for Coyote and themselves. I could not sing there. I wanted to keep on running. I wanted to run high up into the mountains, high above the snow line... I saw children sitting on railroad tracks, in the snow, very sad... they were like sad little warriors in the snow...

(SPIDER WOMAN takes off the gravity a little.)

TRICKSTER: And then I heard the voice of Earth Mother. I knew that I would live. "Balance and breathing," she said, "balance and breathing, and you'll live for sure, Trickster." So I kept on swimming through the bedrock. Then I remembered Old Spider Woman. "Trickster," she said, "when you get to the place of Earth Mother, if there are no children playing, then don't go in there. That means she will be in a very bad mood, and you will never come back. But if there are children playing, then go on in, it's all right. Then you will come back, Trickster, back through the bedrock. And it will be hard but don't give up. You will hear a chant, and the chant is, 'The shadow is ripening, the shadow ripens.' This will help you. So don't be afraid."

COYOTE: It was that Old Spider Woman who fooled around with the gravity! She's made a trap for Coyote! *(Stalks a moment, then, to TRICKSTER)* By the way, don't give anyone my address or phone number. *(Stalks, pauses)* And don't try and take advantage of my great reputation as a warrior by mentioning my name around. *(Stalks)* That old bitch is around here someplace! If I catch her, I will have intercourse with her! I haven't had intercourse in a long time! I've been too busy running!

(Fighting the weight of gravity, and oblivious to everything else, COYOTE continues to search for SPIDER WOMAN, slowly getting himself entangled in her web stage right.)

SPIDER WOMAN: Trickster, I put the gravity on to help you remember. Have you forgotten?

TRICKSTER: Yes... No! I was sent to Earth Mother to ask a question!

SPIDER WOMAN: What was the question?

TRICKSTER: When I got to the place of Earth Mother, after swimming very hard and overcoming every obstacle, there were no children playing. I got so scared that I ran away and hid in a cave. I don't know how long I sat in that cave. There was no Time in that cave. Then I heard the sounds of children playing and singing, so I came out. But meanwhile, I had forgotten the question. So I said, "Earth Mother, where have all the buffalo gone?"

SPIDER WOMAN: And what did she answer?

TRICKSTER: She said that they were in the Land of the Dead.

SPIDER WOMAN: And when will they return, so that the people can live?

TRICKSTER: In the next world. *(Pause)*

SPIDER WOMAN: In the next world... *(For CLOWN and the Audience)* In the First World, the people understood themselves. In his heart man felt the good of life, its sincere purpose. He was of one heart. The First People knew no sickness. But there were those who permitted evil feelings to enter. They were said to be of two hearts. Not until Evil entered the world did persons get sick in the body or the mind... The First World was destroyed by fire...

COYOTE: *(Breaking out of the "web")* Trickster, come out of there and help me find that Old Spider Woman! I want to have intercourse with her!

TRICKSTER: Coyote, come and pull me out of here and then I'll help you! Earth Mother has scraped away my youth! It is too difficult for me!

COYOTE: No! It's a trick! You'll drag me down into the world of the Ant People!

SPIDER WOMAN: *(Continuing)* In the Second World, the people built homes and villages and trails. They made things with their hands and stored food like the Ant People. They could see and talk to each other from the center on top of the head, because this door was still open. Everything they needed was in this Second World, but they began to want more. That was when the trouble started. They forgot to sing joyful praises to the Creator and began singing praises to their goods. This world was turned upside down. It stopped rotating and turned to ice.

COYOTE: I had to make a great effort in those days! I had to get the world turning again! I had to turn it right side up and get it rotating again in its proper place!

SPIDER WOMAN AND TRICKSTER: Coyote had nothing to do with it!

COYOTE: And then I brought a message from Taiowa: First, respect me and one another. And second, sing in harmony from the tops of the hills. When I do not hear you singing from the tops of the hills, I will know you have gone back to evil again. *(To TRICKSTER)* So you can come out of that Ant hill now! *(TRICKSTER throws dirt at him.)*

SPIDER WOMAN: Trickster!

TRICKSTER: In the Third World they advanced rapidly and built big cities!, countries!, a whole civilization! They got preoccupied! Some of them had the power to fly through the air on a shield made of hide!

COYOTE: Coyote can do that to this day! Only he don't need no stinking shield!

TRICKSTER: They could fly around and attack one another. So war and corruption came to this world too. That's why the world has to be destroyed once in a while, so we could have a fresh start. This particular world was destroyed by water.

SPIDER WOMAN: I had to save the people who were not yet cynical, sly, envious, lying sonsabitches! It was ME who saved them! The world was flooded! But to those who were not yet shifty-eyed, smart-assed, negative creeps, I said, "You must continue traveling on. Your inner wisdom will guide you. The door at the top of your head is still open, and your spirits will guide you."

SPIDER WOMAN AND TRICKSTER: *(As TRICKSTER, struggling against old age and the pull of gravity, tries to rise out of the hole.)* The name of this Fourth World is World Complete. It is not all beautiful and easy like the previous ones. It has height and depth, heat and cold, beauty and barrenness. It has everything for you to choose from, but it's up to you to carry out the plan of creation. And if you don't want to, I'll start all over again. You will have help from the proper deities, from your good spirits. Just keep your doors open and remember what I have told you.

COYOTE: (*Pounding his head.*) I knew all that already! (*TRICKSTER falls back into the hole.*) I knew all that already! I knew all that already! (*Pause*) I know what I'll do, I'll ask my little sister where the Spider Lady is. (*Aside to TRICKSTER*) I'm gonna fuck the old broad's brain's out. (*He takes the plant posture*) Little sister...?

(*SPIDER WOMAN steps into the space and challenges COYOTE*)

SPIDER WOMAN: Here I am, Coyote!

COYOTE: Ha! (*He bends over, pointing his anus at her, ready to fire. She kicks him. COYOTE falls over, as if dead. SPIDER WOMAN steps center stage.*)

SPIDER WOMAN: That sky is too far up there. A person can't see the stars. (*She does the "bringing the sky down" movement, causing the strings of Christmas lights in the trees to come on. COYOTE wakes up and starts hitting and berating his anus.*)

COYOTE: You stupid anus! You are not my brother! You are a useless weapon! I don't need you anymore! Etc. (*He collapses from the effort, looks up and notices the "stars."*) I did that! That's MY work!

TRICKSTER: Spider Grandmother, Coyote said that if you would fix the gravity around here, he would have intercourse with you.

COYOTE: I never said that.

SPIDER WOMAN: (*Tempted*) Well... I don't know... it takes a lot of power. Earth Mother is not feeling well, her axis is under a lot of strain. And besides, the moon is wobbling... but if Coyote will have intercourse with me, I might be able to fix it for a while. (*She makes the "taking off the gravity" movement. Trickster—very old—scrambles out of the ground as fast as he can. SPIDER WOMAN lies down expectantly.*)

COYOTE: Wait a minute. I'm not ready.

SPIDER WOMAN: Why not? Let's go!

COYOTE: No, you can't rush these things. These are delicate matters. I have to talk it over with my member. *(SPIDER WOMAN sighs impatiently, while COYOTE addresses his penis. TRICKSTER speaks for COYOTE'S member.)* Little brother?

TRICKSTER: Yes?

COYOTE: Are you in the mood for intercourse?

TRICKSTER: No.

COYOTE: I think you better get ready. The Spider Lady is waiting. I think you are too soft now.

TRICKSTER: I'm not in the mood.

COYOTE: I think you should get in the mood pretty quick, or she'll put the gravity back on.

TRICKSTER: I don't care. I'm not in the mood. I think she has sharp stones in there. You better send someone in there with hammer and chisel first.

COYOTE: I don't like the way you're acting. You're going to get me in a lot of trouble.

TRICKSTER: You can't tell me what to do. I am an independent person. I'm not a two-hearts, like some people. If I'm not in the mood, I'm not in the mood.

COYOTE: I'm bigger than you, so you act the way I tell you to, or...

TRICKSTER: Or what?

COYOTE: I'll cut you off and feed you to the birds.

TRICKSTER: Go ahead. But I ain't goin' in there. If I go in there, I'll never get out again.

COYOTE: *(To SPIDER WOMAN)* He won't do it. *(SPIDER WOMAN gets to her feet.)*

SPIDER WOMAN: *(Laughing)* I've never been so insulted in all my life!

TRICKSTER: *(With a sigh)* Women.

COYOTE: There's nothing I can do. Sometimes he wants to, and sometimes he doesn't.

SPIDER WOMAN: Too bad. *(She puts the gravity back on)* Now I've no desire anyway. For a minute there I forgot what a dope you are.

COYOTE: If you take the gravity off, I'll give you a drink of wine.

SPIDER WOMAN: What's it made of?

COYOTE: Many dead little children. They're fermented now. I've been running and I forgot them.

SPIDER WOMAN: You are an idiot, Coyote. *(She returns to her throne.)*

COYOTE: Actually, it's made of pure Rocky Mountain Spring Water.

TRICKSTER: I'll have some, I've been working my ass off!

COYOTE: Help yourself. *(They drink.)* Uh, oh.

TRICKSTER: This is good. What's the trouble now?

COYOTE: I forgot that I beat up my anus and threw it away.

TRICKSTER: Boy, that was stupid.

COYOTE: How about letting me have YOUR plumbing apparatus?

TRICKSTER: What'll you give me for it?

COYOTE: What do you want?

TRICKSTER: I want to be young and strong and feel the urge for intercourse.

COYOTE: Coyote can do that, but the gravity is in the way.

TRICKSTER: Let's fight the gravity and then I'll decide.

COYOTE: I can't fight without my little brother, the anus, my little brother, the large intestine.

TRICKSTER: Okay. I don't need my large intestine. I'm an old man. I'll loan it to you while we fight the gravity.

COYOTE: It's a deal. *(They do the sound and movement indicating "exchange of the large intestine.")* Good.

TRICKSTER: Now let's prepare to fight the gravity.

COYOTE: First we have to ask the gods for help.

TRICKSTER: Let's go, then!

(They start to move, but SPIDER WOMAN has intensified the gravity. They can hardly walk.)

TRICKSTER: I think this is too much work now. We might as well sit down. It'll save a lot of energy.

COYOTE: Right. *(They settle themselves around the can of sterno.)*

TRICKSTER: That woman is being mean.

COYOTE: I think some women are good for some things, some women are good for other things, and some women are good for nothing... And some women...

(CLOWN sneaks downstage and crouches so that she can overhear COYOTE and TRICKSTER.)

TRICKSTER: I'm a traveling man myself, I haven't had too much time for women.

COYOTE: Let me enlighten you. I remember, for instance, Emily, from Berkeley. She always wore work shirts and she had the most beautiful breasts I have seen to this day. Heh, heh, her boyfriend was a very bad sport. He slashed my tires. Emily... she gave great head. *(Pause)* Margo of Ann Arbor was an interesting person. She appeared at my side while I was practicing running. She stayed with me for two days. She never spoke, but she could have intercourse while running. *(TRICKSTER is amazed.)* Then she looked away for a moment — and there was her ride to the West Coast, waiting.

TRICKSTER: While running?

COYOTE: *(Nodding sagely)* While running. You would have loved Crazy Chrome Faced Woman. She lived in a hut and collected hubcaps. We became good friends. She had the most extensive collection of hubcaps in North America. She was as fearless as Coyote. She could grab a hubcap off a moving car. And Cho Min, who sincerely liked men. In fact, she trusted them, especially Coyote. And Connie of Chimayo, who danced so fast that the raindrops never touched her. But most of all, I remember... *(Sobbing)* I remember She Who Could Not Be Named, who was Coyote's one True Wife. She was there when I left, and there when I came back. No big hellos, no big goodbyes. No smiles, no sighs. Not too much enthusiasm. Light-hearted. Encouraging. And she boiled my buffalo meat just right, and baked wonderfully thin tortillas... This woman was impeccable. From this woman, Coyote learned the meaning of happiness... *(Weeps)*

TRICKSTER: Why are you so sad, Coyote?

COYOTE: This woman, my wife, is in the Land of the Dead now. *(Pause. COYOTE is inconsolable, arousing SPIDER WOMAN's sympathy.)*

SPIDER WOMAN: Are you crying for your lost woman, Coyote?

COYOTE: Yes. I long for her. There is a great pain in my heart.

SPIDER WOMAN: Coyote, your pain is one-hearted. I have taken pity on you. *(TRICKSTER stands and becomes "Spirit of the Dead.")*

TRICKSTER AND SPIDER WOMAN: I can take you to the place where your wife has gone, but you must do exactly as I say. Don't make any foolish mistakes.

COYOTE: Well, what do you expect? Of course, I will do whatever you say!

TRICKSTER: Well, then let's go. *(They start for "The Land of the Dead.")*

COYOTE: *(To TRICKSTER)* I can't see you. You are like a shadow on a dark day.

TRICKSTER: Look at all those horses! It must be a roundup!

COYOTE: *(Pretending)* Oh, yes! Look at all the horses! *(They continue on.)* Must be a roundup!

TRICKSTER: We're almost there. Your wife is in a long lodge here. Wait here and I'll find out exactly. *(He walks around the space, returns to COYOTE.)* Okay, I know where your wife is. *(They mime entering the lodge.)* Sit down here by your wife. *(SPIDER WOMAN, enshrouded, has become COYOTE's wife.)*

COYOTE: I can't see her. She is like a shadow on a dark day.

TRICKSTER: She has prepared our food. Let's eat. *(They mime eating.)* Now, you stay here. I have to go around and say hello to some people. *(He goes about saying hello to members the Audience-- by looking at them directly-- and then returns to COYOTE.)*

COYOTE: Spirit of the Dead, I still can't see my wife! What should I do?

TRICKSTER: Listen, and I will advise you. You must travel five mountains to the West. Your wife will be with you. Slowly, the shadow will ripen. But do not yield to some notion you may have to do something foolish. Do not touch her. When you have crossed the fifth mountain, you can do what you want.

COYOTE: That's the way it'll be then!

(COYOTE rises. His "wife" rises with him and follows. They go back through "The Land of the Dead.")

COYOTE: Look at all those horses! It must be a roundup! *(He looks about for a reply. Silence. He still can't see her. They come back into the space.)*

TRICKSTER: I hope he does everything right, and takes his wife back from the other world. This is the fourth mountain. *(Pause)* The shadow is ripening... the shadow ripens...

(COYOTE and SPIDER WOMAN approach. He begins to see her. For a moment he stands transfixed.)

SPIDER WOMAN: Coyote, do not touch me!

(But COYOTE can't help himself and grabs for her. SPIDER WOMAN, furious, throws off her shroud.)

SPIDER WOMAN: Coyote! You Idiot! You were told not to do anything foolish! We could have established the practice of returning from the Land of the Dead! Now it will never be so! You have ruined it! *(She returns to her throne.)*

COYOTE: No! No! Wait! *(Crazed with grief, he races back through "the Land of the Dead.")* Look at all those horses! It must be a roundup! *(He rushes back into the space. He sits down across from TRICKSTER and mimes eating. He becomes very sad.)*

TRICKSTER: Coyote listened for the voices. He looked all around, but nothing happened. Coyote sat there in the middle of the prairie. He sat there all night, but the lodge did not appear again. In the morning, he heard meadowlarks...

SPIDER WOMAN: *(Gently)* Coyote/Trickster, you have done a terrible thing. But your doors are still open. I have compassion for you. You must turn to your good deities with one-heartedness. If you can do this, I will take off the gravity.

(Separately and then together, COYOTE and TRICKSTER approach the deities one-heartedly. SPIDER WOMAN takes off the gravity.)

TRICKSTER: *(Quickly)* Coyote, I'm tired of all this hard work. I've decided to get a job as a Buffalo for a while. What are you going to do?

COYOTE: I'm going to the Upper World. I think the stars are cruel. I'm going up there to fix them.

TRICKSTER: Well, goodbye.

COYOTE: Good luck, Trickster.

(They shake hands. TRICKSTER runs off. COYOTE looks at the sky, then races up the hill. SPIDER WOMAN steps into the space.)

SPIDER WOMAN: This is the Fourth World... *(Sigh)* ...the World Complete... but Earth Mother has said that things are getting too hard for her... I'm going to move the sky back up. It's too close now.

(She makes the "Moving the Sky" gesture. The lights go out.)

END

III: PLANET OF THE SPIDER PEOPLE

"I can't see!" COYOTE (Darrell Larson) on the *Planet of the Spider People*.

THE SCENE: An enclosed, densely wooded space. Large, hairy SPIDERS are everywhere—in webs, on the ground, hanging from the trees, etc. —and they are ambient, able to move on cue. There are also two large "rocks," one with Buffalo horns sticking out of it. CLOWN, masquerading as a "spider person," hides behind the rock without horns. When the spiders move, she hops about in terror and hides. She is not supposed to be in this place. When the Audience is settled, COYOTE, distraught, eyes tightly closed, crawls down a tree.

COYOTE: Trickster! Trickster! Where are you? I'm lost, Trickster! I don't know where I am! *(He inadvertantly brushes against something and gets a shock.)* Ahhhh! Everything is electrified in this place! Oh, no! Trickster, come up! Come up, Trickster! *(Silence)* Oh, I'm lost and sad! Ahhhh! I'm tired of being sad! I'm tired of being lonely! I can't see! And everything is electrified here!

(TRICKSTER talks from inside the big rock with two buffalo horns sticking out.)

TRICKSTER: Hey, Coyote! Stop complaining so loud! You'll wake up all the people!

COYOTE: Who's talking here?

TRICKSTER: Me! You're not the first person who ever had a hard time of it, so stop feeling sorry for yourself and be quiet!

COYOTE: I'll yell if I want to! I'll talk if I want to! I am Coyote! I have come up here to fix the stars!

TRICKSTER: Why?

COYOTE: Because there is too much suffering down there!

TRICKSTER: I wouldn't take it personally. From up here it doesn't look like shit or shinola.

COYOTE: I don't like your attitude! I think I'll kill you! *(He flounders around making threatening noises.)*

TRICKSTER: Hey Coyote! If you promise to stop making so much noise, I'll tell you where you are.

COYOTE: Coyote knows where he is! Coyote is among the stars! I was on my way to straighten things out up here when some evil, tricky person threw dust in my eyes! I think it was that Old Spider Woman! Otherwise, Coyote would have taken care of things already! He'd have done his task and gone back to his own tribe!

TRICKSTER: Calm yourself, Coyote. If you sit where I tell you, you won't get a shock and you'll find out where you are.

COYOTE: Very well, then. Coyote will sit down.

TRICKSTER: *(Directing him)* Not there! Over there! Now... dig!

(COYOTE digs, discovers a "Milky Way" candy bar.)

COYOTE: Ah! Food! *(He eats.)* You grow good food around here!

TRICKSTER: I never touch the stuff. It's bad for the teeth.

COYOTE: I like 'em better frozen. But thanks a lot, anyway. Thanks a lot.

TRICKSTER: You're welcome.

COYOTE: I still can't see anything. Tell me what my home country looks like, the planet Earth.

TRICKSTER: We don't call it "Earth" up here. We call it Sakasakasaka.

COYOTE: What does that mean?

TRICKSTER: Little Blue Mother Turning in Space.

COYOTE: Is my mother's color blue?

TRICKSTER: Most of the time. That's the main impression of her. Blue. And she has a little yellow guy turning with her. He's called Babababababa.

COYOTE: And what does that mean?

TRICKSTER: Little Blue Mother's Yellow Little Kid.

COYOTE: Can you see any of my brothers and sisters?

TRICKSTER: No.

COYOTE: Any human beings?

TRICKSTER: No. *(A sort of telescope protrudes from the rock's "head.")* I see thousands of immense clouds of gas and dust! These are the most massive objects in this galaxy! And these great clouds are held together by their own self-gravity! Each one of these things is worth about a hundred thousand suns!

COYOTE: Where?

TRICKSTER: You can't see them. They don't radiate any light. And nobody knows what's holding 'em up there in the first place. *(The telescope retracts.)* If I were you, I wouldn't strain myself in that direction. I'd use my energy to watch out for the Spider People.

COYOTE: *(Leaping to his feet)* The Spider People! You got Spider People here?

TRICKSTER: I heard of some Spider People around here talking about killing you.

COYOTE: Oh, no!

TRICKSTER: I'll go and find out what they are going to do.

COYOTE: Okay! But come back soon! *(The rock moves a few inches to the right and all the spiders move also.)* Creature? Creature?

TRICKSTER: That was another one, a cousin of mine. But I'll tell you something good. Why do you think the Spider Lady hangs around in a tree? What do you think about that?

COYOTE: I don't know what to think.

TRICKSTER: She holds on to the tree and shuts her eyes and she can see everything over the whole Milky Way. This tree here is the Chief of the whole Milky Way. That is why spiders always go on trees.

COYOTE: This is news to me.

TRICKSTER: Do you wish to see everything, or not?

COYOTE: Certainly, I do!

TRICKSTER: Well, keep your eyes shut, hold onto this tree and you will see everything!

COYOTE: I'll try it. *(He touches the tree and gets a shock.)* Ahhhh! You tricked me, Creature! You tricked me! I'll kill you!

TRICKSTER: I forgot a part. I'm sorry. Rub your feet on the ground three times and you won't get a shock. You'll like it very much.

(COYOTE rubs his feet, touches the tree, then leaps into the tree and throws his arms around it.)

COYOTE: Oh, I love this tree! I love this tree! This tree is a true Chief! *(The Spider People move around. TRICKSTER stands, shedding his rock outfit. He wears a Buffalo Robe and a Buffalo headpiece.)* I can see! I can see over the whole Milky Way! I can see the four elements! I can see the four directions! I can see above and below! I can see the beginning and the end! I can see in the middle! And it is...! It is...!

TRICKSTER: Don't open your eyes, Coyote! *(COYOTE opens his eyes. The SPIDER PEOPLE bustle about. COYOTE howls)*

COYOTE: Did I see that? Did I see that?

TRICKSTER: What?

COYOTE: *(Jumping out of the tree)* My brother the Buffalo, are you really there?

TRICKSTER: Where?

COYOTE: Don't be an idiot! This is Coyote talking! Are you in front of my eyes or behind my eyes?

TRICKSTER: That question is too thick for me. I can't understand it.

TRICKSTER (Norbert Weisser), wearing his Buffalo robe and headdress, and COYOTE (Darrell Larson) evade Spider People.

COYOTE: My brother the Buffalo, are there Spider People here, too?

TRICKSTER: I think there are Spider People here, too.

COYOTE: My brother, the Buffalo, is there a creature here with a bad attitude?

TRICKSTER: Coyote, I don't see a creature here with a bad attitude.

COYOTE: My brother the Buffalo, if you are really here too, then let's go back to our own tribe.

TRICKSTER: How will we get there?

COYOTE: I will ride there in the hump of your back.

TRICKSTER: There is no hump on my back here, Coyote.

COYOTE: Then I will ride inside you, Buffalo. I will ride in your entrails.

TRICKSTER: There is no room for you in there, Coyote, because I loaned my large intestine to a two-hearted person.

COYOTE: That was a stupid thing to do! Coyote can't get back to his own tribe now!

(The voice of SPIDER WOMAN is heard from within the other large rock.)

SPIDER WOMAN: Oh, the shame of the eyeballs! The horror of the feet!

TRICKSTER: There is a creature here with a bad attitude.

(The SPIDER PEOPLE make a ruckus. COYOTE and TRICKSTER head for the trees.)

SPIDER WOMAN: You see that? You can't make a move around here without stepping on something.

COYOTE: *(Clinging to the tree)* My brother the Buffalo — who is this guy?

TRICKSTER: Hey, Creature — are you a bona fide Indian or a two-hearted white-eyes?

SPIDER WOMAN: What difference does it make? I'm a person!

TRICKSTER: What tribe?

SPIDER WOMAN: Shmohawk.

TRICKSTER: Maybe we know that tribe. Where do they make camp? We could be relatives of yours!

COYOTE: I never heard of that tribe!

SPIDER WOMAN: When I was a Shmohawk down there I never knew what was happening. Sit down, Buffalo Head. You're making me nervous.

TRICKSTER: I'm afraid of the Spider People.

SPIDER WOMAN: They won't bother you as long as I'm talking.

TRICKSTER: Keep on talking, Creature.

COYOTE: Keep on talking!

SPIDER WOMAN: Well, we didn't know shit from shinola. Thirty-five miles up and nothing exists down there. There's no surface on the surface. No cities, no mountains, no lights, no freeways. And from up here? Just a little blue marble spinning in the light of the sun. (*She stops. Movement from the SPIDER PEOPLE.*)

COYOTE AND TRICKSTER: Talk, Creature!

SPIDER WOMAN: I acted like I knew what I was doing. All us Shmohawks did. We thought we knew about the stars and planets and atoms and molecules and galaxies and what everything meant. It's frustrating. You don't know when to watch it, when to leave it alone. You don't know if it's ever all right. It's not your fault, but you're responsible. It is your fault, but you're too hard on yourself. You're damned if you do, and damned if you don't. I got sent up here with all these Spiders because I'm the type which is afraid of stepping on things. But you can watch it just so long, and then — whoops, you've done it again. (*She pauses. Movement from the SPIDER PEOPLE.*) You try and stop one thing and another one starts, worse than before. You pay your taxes, and they audit you. You stop smoking and you bloat up. You give up drinking and you find yourself with a taste for kinky sex. You give up sex and you get manic depressive, laughing or crying all the time. You're too loud or too quiet and your own presence is a torture to yourself and a burden to others. To sum up, I think the worst thing about being a Shmohawk is: you have no idea what you're doing, but you have to pay the consequences anyway, and then you resent it.

COYOTE AND TRICKSTER: Those poor Shmohawks!

SPIDER WOMAN: And then — Bang! You end up here on the Planet of the Spider People!

COYOTE AND TRICKSTER: Oh, no!

SPIDER WOMAN: Look into my eyes, Coyote/Trickster, and tell what you see.

(*They peer at the Rock Creature.*)

COYOTE: Your eyes are full of pain, Creature!

TRICKSTER: Your eyes are showing a lot of fear, Creature!

SPIDER WOMAN: It's because I have to stay in here and not move. If I come out of here, I might say something, I might do something, I might step on something. But the real horror of it all is – everything is ordinary. Everything just has to be done. I get up. I groan. I brush my teeth. I throw water on my face. Of course, it's not water like on Earth, but same difference. Then I get dressed. In clothes. Then I cook and eat. Spider People breakfast. Not like on Earth, but same difference. I read the paper. Spider People News. Then I go to the bathroom. *(Sound of toilet flushing inside the rock.)* Not like on Earth, but same difference. And so on.

TRICKSTER: I know exactly how you feel, Creature! A long time ago Coyote and I made a vow to Earthmaker to never, ever touch a woman again — especially if she was young and beautiful. One day, after prospecting in the mountain canyons for gold, we decided to go into town for a drink. It had been raining for weeks and the roads were all mud. When we got into town, the stagecoach had just arrived — and there in that coach was the most beautiful damsel I had ever laid my eyes on! Long blonde hair, blue eyes, the prettiest smile you ever seen, a blue cotton dress, parasol over her arm, and as she was trying to step out of that coach she lifted her dress up a little, like this... ah... But, of course she couldn't move, because the street was overflowing with mud.

SPIDER WOMAN: Is this conversation nearly over?

TRICKSTER: Well, before I could say "bip," Coyote was over there, picked her up and carried her across the muddy road into the saloon, put her down on the bar and bought her a drink! The cowboys were whoopin' and laughin'. I was stunned! I didn't know what to think! I couldn't say a word! I couldn't even drink that night! While Coyote was downing one brandy after another! Days later back at the camp I finally asked him, "Coyote!" I says, "Coyote! How could you do such a thing, after making that vow to Earthmaker?" Do you know what he said?

COYOTE: Are you still carrying her? I put her down days ago!

SPIDER WOMAN: That story is too thick for me. I can't understand it.

COYOTE: Try to follow this. One day the Coyote and the Trickster needed a judgement made. So they went to Earthmaker. And Earthmaker made his judgement, but the Trickster did not agree with the judgement. So do you know what he did? He put his shoes on top of his head and he walked out of the room!

SPIDER WOMAN: Hey, Coyote, I think I hear your mother calling!

COYOTE: My brother the Buffalo, I feel sorry for this guy.

TRICKSTER: Watch out, Coyote. This is an old trick. This creature has a bad attitide.

COYOTE: My brother the Buffalo, maybe if we help this creature with a bad attitude, we'll be able to go back to our own tribe. Hey, Creature.

SPIDER WOMAN: What?

COYOTE: You got a sun up here?

SPIDER WOMAN: No, I don't have a wife here. It's better that way. If I had a son, he'd grow up to be just like me.

COYOTE: I didn't mean that! I meant the sun in the sky! When the sun rises, you start all over again! That's Coyote's way!

SPIDER WOMAN: The sun won't rise here for another million years, Coyote. One million years here is one sunrise. (*Pause*)

COYOTE: I know what I'll do!

SPIDER WOMAN: What's that?

COYOTE: I'll turn myself into a woman and become your wife! That way you can start something new!

TRICKSTER: Wait, Coyote! (*COYOTE turns himself into a woman. To Audience*) Coyote turned himself into a woman. He was always doing crazy things like that. That's because Coyote had no limits. When the sun rose on Earth, he started over. He forgot all about it. It was all brand new for him...

SPIDER WOMAN: Hey, Miss Coyote — you are a beautiful woman. You really turn me on. My heart is pounding and my member is pulsing. I can think of nothing but you. I can't live without you. In short, I feel romantic.

COYOTE: That's what they said back in my own tribe. All the young men wanted to marry me. I had to go away from there, because I wasn't attracted to any of those young men.

TRICKSTER: Hey, Coyote — why don't you come into MY lodge? We'll spend the night fooling around. You'll find it very agreeable.

COYOTE: No! I'm not attracted to you! Besides, my heart belongs to another person. He is different than the rest of you. He is an extraordinary person! He's quite a guy!

TRICKSTER: He can't hunt! He can't fish! And he's afraid of stepping on things. He'll have a lot of trouble making a living.

COYOTE: I don't care. He is very sensitive. And Coyote can go kill a hundred rabbits anytime she wants to. She will do anything for her man!

SPIDER WOMAN: Don't listen to him, Miss Coyote, and come into MY lodge.

COYOTE: I want to, Mr. Creature, but only if your intentions are honorable. You shouldn't take advantage of an innocent girl.

SPIDER WOMAN: I hadn't intended marriage. But I'm in love, so if that's the way it is, then that's the way it is. I want to have you for my wife, Miss Coyote, because I think you're terrific. I'm pretty shy, though. I don't have much experience in these matters.

COYOTE: Let's get married and have kids, Mr. Creature. I find you extremely attractive, so don't worry about that other stuff. Coyote will show you how it's done.

TRICKSTER: (To Audience) Coyote and the Creature tied the knot... and retired to their lodge... Coyote was a good wife... (COYOTE mimes.) She prepared his food... she sewed his moccasins... she fed his horses... she hunted rabbits... she washed his clothes... she decorated the lodge... she arranged a dinner party for a week from Thursday... she made his bed... and lay down in it to await her husband... the Creature was very pleased... *(SPIDER WOMAN belches.)*

SPIDER WOMAN: Now I'll go in to my wife...

TRICKSTER: At first Coyote couldn't find the Creature's member, because it was in a funny place, but then she got a shock.

COYOTE: Oh! You're electrified!

SPIDER WOMAN: I'm sorry. I forgot to tell you. Rub your feet three times. You won't get a shock. You'll like it very much.

(COYOTE rubs his feet three times, then has "intercourse" with the rock.)

TRICKSTER: Coyote liked it very much. She got pregnant right away.

SPIDER WOMAN: Thank you, Miss Coyote. You're the first woman that ever cared for me as a person. I feel much better about myself. I don't feel so insecure now. In fact, I feel strong enough to go back down there and try again.

COYOTE: But Mr. Creature, you can't leave now — I am pregnant!

(SPIDER WOMAN stands, shedding her rock costume. She is dressed like a man in suit and tie.)

SPIDER WOMAN: I'm sorry, Coyote, but you knew it wasn't serious. You knew it couldn't last. These things happen. I can't let it ruin my life. I have to get myself together now. I'm gonna clean up my act, avoid entanglements, keep my mouth shut, and try not to step on anything. *(Seeing CLOWN)* What are you doing here, you little twirp! Are you trying to destroy my trick? Go over there and make yourself useful. *(Grabs CLOWN by the ear and propels her toward COYOTE, who is about to give birth on the side of a knoll.)* The Earth isn't such a bad place to live. Same difference, but what the hell. I can make it. Mainly because I don't give a rat's ass. I'm not one of you guys and I never will be, heh, heh. *(She straightens her tie and exits through the Audience, trying not to step on anything.)*

TRICKSTER: *(To Audience)* The Creature went back to being a Shmohawk again.

COYOTE: Oh! Oh!

TRICKSTER: Coyote was in labor. But the kids wouldn't come out. Hey, Coyote — it's time to give birth now! You got plenty kids in there!

COYOTE: Oh! That's what you get for trying to help a guy out! Coyote was very foolish to fall for that guy! Oh! One night of temptation! One night of pleasure! And look what happens to a person! Look what happens! And who is gonna take care of the kids now? Oh! Coyote is sorry he became a woman!

TRICKSTER: Hey, Coyote — you're in a fine pickle! Maybe I'll give you a hand getting those kids out!

COYOTE: Oh! My brother the Buffalo, if you give Coyote a hand pushing these kids out of me, we will go to all the tribes and tell them what a great guy you are, and then they won't kill you for your meat!

TRICKSTER: *(To Audience)* I knew that Coyote would forget all about it, but I decided to help him anyway. Otherwise he would keep on yelling. *(Goes to COYOTE)* Hey, Coyote — the kids can't come out of there because there's no door there. I'll have to make a door, and then the kids will come out.

COYOTE: Oh! My brother the Buffalo — make a door! *(TRICKSTER makes a door.)*

TRICKSTER: Okay you kids — come on out of there! *(Pause. He puts his ear to the door.)* First-born, they won't come out!

COYOTE: My brother the Buffalo, why won't they come out?

TRICKSTER: They don't have any names. They're afraid to come out without a name. If you give them a name, they'll come out.

COYOTE: How can I give them a name if I don't know who they are? I never heard of anything so stupid! When I see how they are, I'll give them a name!

TRICKSTER: They say that you are the true Chief and Father of their tribe, so you should give them each a name. Then they'll come out.

COYOTE: How many of 'em are there?

(TRICKSTER motions CLOWN to take a look. CLOWN crawls half-way inside, returns and shows "twelve" with her fingers.)

TRICKSTER: Twelve.

COYOTE: Let's go then! *(CLOWN helps "midwife" the following births.)*

COYOTE AND TRICKSTER: Oh! "Takes It All Back because He Didn't Mean It." *(A Spider Baby runs out of COYOTE.)* Oh! "Pretends He Is Thinking Of Something Else." *(Another Spider)* Oh! "Looks At His Hand With Profound Interest." *(Another Spider)* Oh! "Turns Away to See What's Happening There." *(Another Spider)* Oh! "Coolly Denies He Is Angry." *(Another Spider)* Oh! "Would Rather Be In New York City." *(Another Spider)* Oh! "Says It's Not His Ego, But Something Real." *(Another Spider)* Oh! "Does You a Favor." "Never Joins The Circle." "Acts Like He Knows What You Mean." "Certain Things He Can't Agree With." *(Four more Spider Babies run out. COYOTE falls back exhausted.)*

COYOTE: Oh! *(Pause)* They got all that stuff from their father. *(He sits up. The SPIDERS all crawl and bounce around. COYOTE and TRICKSTER scream, rush to the trees and throw their arms around them.)*

COYOTE AND TRICKSTER: *(As lost little boys)* Spider Grandmother! Please! Help us get back to our own tribe!

(A huge straw model of one of the figurines from Coyote I: Pointing *rises up some distance off, its eyes flashing. COYOTE and TRICKSTER get a shock from the trees and fall to the ground, cowering in fear. SPIDER WOMAN's voice is heard as if coming from everywhere.)*

SPIDER WOMAN: Coyote/Trickster, you thought you could climb up here and fix things. That was your shadow talking. I had to throw star dust in your eyes. In this way you got lost and you don't know what's real anymore. You even thought you could become a woman. And so your Earthly Mother is ashamed, First-born, and the stars above are turned cold against you. Earthmaker hopes you have learned a lesson from all this.

COYOTE AND TRICKSTER: *(As little boys)* But Spider Grandmother, when can I go back to my own tribe? And how will I get there?

SPIDER WOMAN: When the sun rises, Coyote/Trickster. When the sun rises...

(COYOTE crawls into TRICKSTER's arms. Darkness.)

END

IV: OTHER SIDE CAMP

L to R: COYOTE (Darrell Larson), TRICKSTER (Norbert Weisser), and SPIDER
WOMAN (Christine Avila) in two-legged walk from *Other Side Camp*.

The CLOWN gathers the Audience, wordlessly encouraging them to follow her. Still mute, she hand signs, gesticulates, writes notes, blows a horn, etc.

CLOWN: Come along! I think we got a chance to see some gods appear!... Follow me, there may be some divinities down there! I'm not kidding!... I heard people say that some gods might come down over there! Let's go see!... Who knows? We might see some gods together! Wouldn't that be terrific? Down there!... I don't know for sure, but I think gods might show up over there! Spread the word!

(She escorts the Audience to the space: a stockaded area in an open field. Upstage are what may be the ruins of an ancient ceremonial city — a set composed of found objects, sandbags, bricks, cement blocks, stones, etc. A few feet below the set, left, stand the bones of a tall, dried-out saguaro tree. Behind it, motionless, stands TRICKSTER, wrapped in a blanket, facing upstage. Across from him, right, is a kind of pylon—wood or metal—perhaps a dolmen we can no longer decipher. Behind it is COYOTE, motionless, wrapped in a blanket. He also faces away from the Audience.)

(The Audience in place, CLOWN enjoins willing members to step forward and say out these speeches, which are hand-lettered on scrolls.)

SCROLL 1: Coyote was supposed to bring the waterfall to earth but he got into a fight with himself and Old Spider Woman had to scare him off. Now everybody's thirsty. If I see him I'm gonna kick him in the knees!

SCROLL 2: Coyote went running around the whole planet. He could see wonderful things but he preferred to fool around with women!

SCROLL 3: Trickster went to the center of the earth on an important mission, but when he got there he couldn't remember what the mission was. And that is why we are all here like this today!

SCROLL 4: I'll tell you another thing Coyote did. He ruined the practice of returning from the Land of the Dead — just because he couldn't control one silly impulse!

SCROLL 5: The thing I can't get over is the time he turned himself into a woman and gave birth to twelve strange spider-people! That was a pisser!

SCROLL 6: I hear that Mr. Coyote/Trickster is behaving very badly now. He is going around like a drunken Indian. He must have a lot of pain in his liver or he wouldn't act like that!

SCROLL 7: Well, that's because Old Spider Woman got mad at him. He doesn't know whether he's "here" or "there" anymore! Let's hope she takes pity on him soon!

(That concluded, CLOWN takes her place — just offstage down right, but in plain view of the Audience — and blows a whistle. COYOTE and TRICKSTER start moving slowly toward one another. They've done some hard traveling.)

COYOTE: Are there any MEN here? *(Pause)*

TRICKSTER: I see a two-legged walker! *(Pause)*

COYOTE: Ha! *(Pause)* I see one who thinks he is a fear-inspiring object! *(Pause)*

TRICKSTER: Ha! *(Pause)* I think you should stay with your Grandmother! *(Pause)*

COYOTE: Ha! *(Pause)* I see one who has slept with too many women of dubious health and uncertain origin! *(Pause)*

TRICKSTER: Ha! *(Pause)* I have in my eyes a two-legged whose pecker has crawled with snakes! *(Pause)*

COYOTE: Ha! *(Pause)* I hear a windpipe which has swallowed all the two-legged substances for the seeing and feeling and warping of reality! *(Pause)*

(They continue hurling ad-lib insults as they approach one another, until, their momentum nearly exhausted, they turn abruptly together to face downstage. A pause.)

COYOTE: Oh! This is something new entirely! *(Pause)*

COYOTE AND TRICKSTER: I am Coyote/Trickster and I want to get back to my own tribe! *(A pause; they begin to move slowly downstage towards the Audience.)*

COYOTE: My skin is burning in this place. My hair is burning. My eyes are burning. My head-bone is burning. I feel that there has been a terrible mistake. I was a happy fellow once, on my home planet, with my own tribe, but then I got on the wrong train.

TRICKSTER: I'm looking for the bones... I'm looking for the bones... I'm looking for the bones in the ground... for the gaps between the bones... the spaces in the bones... the lines and markings, the contours of the bones... I'm looking for the life on earth... the life moving around in the ground, in the earth...

COYOTE: I took the Coney Island Local but I ended up in Seagate. Hundreds of us dumped at the planet's edge, beach and causeways in an orange haze. I heard the SLAP of the ocean. I lay down in the sun.

TRICKSTER: My feet are burning. The stones are burning. The seeds are burning. The stones under the stones are burning. The gravel is burning. The sand is burning. The water in the marrow of my bones is burning.

COYOTE: My body got brown and warm. I ate a hot dog. I had no identification. My bowels were burning. I could see Sheepshead. I could see England. I could see the back of my skull.

TRICKSTER: The wind is burning. The trees are burning. My voice is burning. The sound is burning. The air is burning. My blanket is burning.

COYOTE: The sun was growing black and the fish were mutating. The ferris wheel was burning. The algae were burning. The sun was turning black.

TRICKSTER: My throat is burning. My breath is burning. My heartbeat is burning.

COYOTE: I wrapped myself in a blanket. I wanted to do a Christ. My blanket was burning. I was eaten alive.

TRICKSTER: My blood is burning. My cells are burning. My atoms are burning.

COYOTE: Night came and the people went away. I built a fire, attracting teenage gangs. I would have killed to protect my fire. The ocean whacked the filthy beach. Vengeance — got to clean up the mess —

COYOTE AND TRICKSTER: IT IS PILING UP BODIES. *(They stop in front of the Audience. Pause.)*

TRICKSTER: What is this here... "happy"?

COYOTE: I didn't do nothin'. I just woke up with it in the morning.

TRICKSTER: Could you say more about that?

COYOTE: I'm trying to remember. I think I had a softball game in the afternoon and a date that night. *(Pause)*

TRICKSTER: What is this here... "local"?

COYOTE: It's a subway.

TRICKSTER: What is this here... "subway"?

COYOTE: It is a very fine sensation. A person can sit still and be moving at the same time.

TRICKSTER: Ha! What is this here... "beach"?

COYOTE: Brighton. Bay One. *(With a fixed stare)* I see a boat out there weighing anchor. It has made no sound. There is no sign on it. Some of the inhabitants have turned against each other. Some are wading out into the water. Some are busy with masts and sails and a flag...

TRICKSTER: Ha!

COYOTE: Ha, what?!

TRICKSTER: That experience is very familiar to me.

COYOTE: So?

TRICKSTER: That experience is more than familiar to me. You stole that experience. That was MY experience.

COYOTE: Don't be an idiot.

TRICKSTER: I am not an idiot! I am a deep person! I am a god! I am Mudhead!

COYOTE: Okay, Mudhead.

TRICKSTER: Right! And I don't want no shallow asshole stealing my deep experiences!

COYOTE: Fine. I don't want no trouble. All I'm trying to do is find my way back to my own tribe.

TRICKSTER: So am I! *(Pause)*

COYOTE: I'll tell you a secret, Mudhead.

TRICKSTER: Yeah? *(Pause)*

COYOTE: I am Coyote!

TRICKSTER: Ha!

COYOTE: Is that all you can think of saying?

TRICKSTER: What?

COYOTE: Ha!

TRICKSTER: Ha! *(TRICKSTER is confused. COYOTE sees a way out.)*

COYOTE: Let's settle up on this thing, Mudhead, so we can go on to something new.

TRICKSTER: What thing?

COYOTE: What will you take in exchange for your experience?

TRICKSTER: *(Thinks it over)* I'll take your blanket. Even Stephen. I'll take your blanket for my experience.

COYOTE: *(Considers)* That sounds fair enough, on the face of it. *(Pause)* So, the first thing is for you to give me an experience. And then I'll give you my blanket.

TRICKSTER: Wait one minute! I already gave you an experience!

COYOTE: I'm sorry, but that doesn't count.

TRICKSTER: Why not? It was a true, bona fide experience!

COYOTE: I don't remember it anymore. Do you?

TRICKSTER: *(Trying)* Something about a boat?

COYOTE: If we don't remember it, then it never happened. We have to start all over again. Certainly you can appreciate that.

TRICKSTER: Of course, I appreciate it!

COYOTE: All right, then. *(Waits)* Come on, we gotta get movin'!

TRICKSTER: Uh, in my dreams, the cloud upon which I walk is full of holes: one for every step I take. *(Pause)*

COYOTE: That's not an experience.

TRICKSTER: What is it then? I thought that was very deep!

COYOTE: It was deep all right, but it wasn't an experience. It was a psychological state.

TRICKSTER: *(Angrily)* Does it have to be in New York City to qualify?

COYOTE: *(Magnaminous)* No. *(Trickster is stumped.)* I have an idea.

TRICKSTER: *(Eagerly)* You do?

COYOTE: Yeah. One blanket equals one experience. All we have to do is exchange blankets. Then we'll be even Stephen.

TRICKSTER: Even Stephen?

COYOTE: You bet.

TRICKSTER: *(Cautiously)* It makes sense...

COYOTE: Then let's exchange blankets. *(An impasse)* I have another idea.

TRICKSTER: Shoot.

COYOTE: Since we already have our blankets, let's not waste our time with exchanging them, and if anyone asks later, we'll just say that we did.

TRICKSTER: What?

COYOTE: Exchanged blankets! *(Pause)*

TRICKSTER: I'll have to think about it. *(Turns away)*

COYOTE: Sure thing. *(Turns away also)*

(SPIDER WOMAN enters upstage center, from the other side of "camp." She is dressed outlandishly and carries a large kettle strapped to her waist. She halts atop the ruins, and sings.)

SPIDER WOMAN: I am Kokyonwuhti!
                I recieve light and nourish life!
                I am Mother of all that shall ever come!

(Taking note of COYOTE and TRICKSTER, she becomes HOMELESS CRAZY WOMAN and steps down into the space.)

SPIDER WOMAN: It's hard to find a place to make camp these days! Time was, for a quarter, you could pull right up to a parking meter and have a nice space of your own for an hour! Now, there was a comfort! *(She stops, sings)*

> Now let the things
> That move
> In the thought of my Lord
> Appear!

COYOTE AND TRICKSTER: *(Menacing)* What's that you say?

SPIDER WOMAN: The Chinaman died seventeen years ago. I went to the morgue to see him and he was under a sheet. There was this stitch on his neck where they put the embalming fluid in. I gave the mortician twenty dollars for flowers but I could tell by the way he looked at me that he put the money into his own pocket. The Chinaman had a good laundry business over there, but all those buildings disappeared a long time ago. We used to have a lot of postmen come in with shirts. The Chinaman got jealous of one of the postmen. I left him twice. I said, "Postmen get lonely just like Chinamen!" I said I was leaving and never coming back. He asked a lady in the lobby where I was, but she didn't know, so he left me a note and it said, "PLEASE COME BACK, I'M SORRY." *(She has moved off behind the tree, left.)*

COYOTE: Who was that?

TRICKSTER: I don't know. But I think she was a good-looking woman.

COYOTE: Do I know her?

TRICKSTER: Who cares? I'd like to fuck her. Do you have any money?

COYOTE: Not for you, I don't.

SPIDER WOMAN: *(Re-enters, singing)*

> The crosspoles are made
> of sky and earth cords,
> the warp-sticks of sun rays,
> the healds of rock crystal and sheet lightning.
> the batten was a sun halo,
> white shell made the comb.

(Speaking matter-of-factly, she turns center stage and starts majestically down towards the Audience. COYOTE and TRICKSTER, entranced, follow on either side of her.)

SPIDER WOMAN: There were four spindles:
one a stick of zigzag lightning
with a whorl of cannel coal;
one a stick of flash lightning
with a whorl of turquoise;
a third had a stick of sheet lightning
with a whorl of abalone;
a rain streamer formed
the stick of the fourth,
and its whorl was a white shell.
The dark blue, yellow and white winds
quickened the spindles according
to their color and enabled them
to travel around the world.

TRICKSTER: That story was very familiar to me, but I can't quite place it in my mind...

SPIDER WOMAN: That was my loom, Sonny. My loom.

COYOTE: *(Alerted)* Your loom?

SPIDER WOMAN: *(As HOMELESS CRAZY WOMAN)* Then, when he was in the hospital with a cancer of the rectum, he said, "Please hang around till I can get up again." I went to visit him but they took him to the convalescent home. He said, "Honey, I don't know what's wrong with me." He kept saying that. I told him, "You'll be all right. You'll be up and walking in your pajamas in a few days." I told him I'd come back. I went back three days later and he was dead. *(To Audience)* Shhh... The Chinese will never be civilized like white people. You can send them to college — Harvard, Oxford, Cal State, whatever— but they're still Chinese! *(Pause)* I sleep real good at night, but it's so hard to get up in the morning. *(She puts down her kettle.)*

TRICKSTER: *(Approaching)* Uh, Lady? You know, I couldn't help but be moved by that experience of yours. I was quite touched by it. And you know, it was a very familiar experience. It reminded me of a time, years ago, while I was on a important mission for Old Spider Woman. I was —

SPIDER WOMAN: What would people do if they didn't gather things all day? Play shuffleboard?

TRICKSTER: *(As if shocked into recognition)* HI!

SPIDER WOMAN: *(Ignoring him)* The most important thing in life is making a good soup. I use last night's stock and the events of the day. I try to be discriminating, but some things are out of my hands. Beggars can't be choosers. I got the mating cry of a wild bus this morning, and one very unusual grimace. Never seen it before on this earth — lust, hunger, and revenge — all mixed up in one face. *(She puts this into her "Soup.")*

COYOTE: Is that what you're doing? Making soup?

SPIDER WOMAN: This is a soup that'll make you wish you had stayed with your *Abuelita*, you CHANGO.

COYOTE: What do you put in it?

SPIDER WOMAN: The songs and the dreams of the gods!

TRICKSTER: What about my experience? I was about to say an experience back there! I, Mudhead, claim ownership of that experience!

COYOTE: *(Taking him aside)* Don't talk to a person when they're busy!

SPIDER WOMAN: *(Making the "Soup")* Three lizard grins... Eleven dead motorcycle exhaust pipes... Four ounces adipose tissue from a forty-two-year-old Mexican junkie... Seven denials... One forty-nine Chevy back seat... A well-scratched-up pew... Two vials of distilled right-wing religious hysteria... Twenty years of advice.... Ten years of waiting for MY check... Twenty five years of feeling guilty for no damn reason... Etc.

COYOTE: Don't take this personally lady, but that is an absolutely disgusting soup!

TRICKSTER: I agree. Nobody in his right mind would eat such a soup!

SPIDER WOMAN: That's where we live, *Chicos.*

COYOTE AND TRICKSTER: *(Charging her)* Where?

SPIDER WOMAN: *(Holding them off)* Now I'll show you something really entertaining! *(She lifts the kettle to reveal an illuminated spidery design inside, then puts it down, sits on it, beams. COYOTE, TRICKSTER and CLOWN applaud politely.)*

TRICKSTER: I'd like to refer back, if I may, to the question of stolen experiences. *(SPIDER WOMAN stands and puts the kettle over her head.)*

COYOTE AND TRICKSTER: *(Startled)* Oh.

COYOTE: *(Venturing)* VIVA CERCA DE AQUI?

SPIDER WOMAN: *(Contemptuous)* MONDE USTED? I don't live here. I live on the other side of town, and my acupuncturist is a complete asshole. I get disability payments. This whole camp is full of crazy people. They can't see reality. As for me, I don't give a rat's ass.

TRICKSTER: You don't?

SPIDER WOMAN: Nope. I don't wanna see reality. Every day I make a new soup and that takes care of that. I put everything into it but the kitchen sink. On the other hand, there are people going hungry in this world.

COYOTE: *(To Trickster)* Maybe now we're getting somewhere.

SPIDER WOMAN: I'm not happy with my soup of the day.

TRICKSTER: *(Discouraged)* Another day, another soup.

SPIDER WOMAN: There's a missing ingredient. A certain substance... I'll make you an offer— you supply the missing ingredient for my soup, and I'll show you the way back to the real world and your own tribe.

COYOTE AND TRICKSTER: What is this here ingredient?

SPIDER WOMAN: It is a watery substance with little fish things in it.

COYOTE: What is this here substance called?

SPIDER WOMAN: Sex. *(An Impasse. COYOTE and TRICKSTER are perplexed.)* Now you have the opportunity to accomplish an interesting experience.

TRICKSTER: *(Pushing COYOTE out of the way)* I'm ready then! *(TRICKSTER is lost. No one moves. Meekly:)* The least you can do is take that kettle off your head.

SPIDER WOMAN: Oh. I'm sorry.

(She shyly takes off the kettle. CLOWN indicates where the kettle should be and SPIDER WOMAN puts it down. Music. TRICKSTER following, she looks for a nice spot and gracefully bends over. TRICKSTER looks at her. He is at a loss. Finally, he decides to do as she does. He bends over facing the opposite direction and backs in so that their buttocks touch. SPIDER WOMAN is amazed. Meanwhile, CLOWN sneaks onstage and pours water and a fish into the kettle. COYOTE notices the new condition of the kettle and rushes over.)

COYOTE: Holy Toledo! A fish! I'll catch that fish! *(He thrashes in the kettle with no success, decides to drink the water. He drinks some of the water and catches the fish in his mouth.)* Aha! I got you! *(He spits the fish away.)* Phooey! This fish is dead! *(Now TRICKSTER and SPIDER WOMAN are "stuck," rump to rump, like dogs.)*

TRICKSTER: Hey, Coyote! This has been a lot of fun, but it's over now! It's time to go on to something else now!

COYOTE: So what do you want from me?

SPIDER WOMAN: We're stuck, stupid!

COYOTE: Oh no! But don't worry! Help is on the way! *(He throws the rest of the water from the kettle on them and they come unstuck.)* There!

TRICKSTER: Thank you very much. That was an interesting experience. For a moment there, I—

COYOTE: Tell us another time! *(A drumbeat, as SPIDER WOMAN majestically shows the four directions. COYOTE, on his knees, addresses the sky.)* That's where I come from! And that is Earthmaker's tent! The sky is the home of thunder, the palace of Taiowa! He comes down here to gather snakes! And if you see fire up there, that means his wings are beating! And if there's a big tumult up there, that means he's brought his kids along!

TRICKSTER: If you want to steal my experiences, then you have to include the people, the life of the people! Let's try and be humble for a change.

COYOTE: I have an idea.

TRICKSTER: What's that?

COYOTE: Let's try and be humble for a change. *(A sneer from TRICKSTER. To SPIDER WOMAN, very fast:)* Is it a question of economics — the value of a dollar — Dictatorship of the Proletariat — too many people on earth — population control — what do I mean? — I mean, being a regular guy, regular, a member of the community, a guy who pays his bills, a guy with money in his pocket, a success! *(SPIDER WOMAN points and a beam of light comes out of the ground at COYOTE's feet. He whirls away.)*

TRICKSTER: *(Fast)* What about this here? — the love of a woman— someone to do my shirts — marriage and a home — a hot meal — a house in the country and three little kids — friendship! One man I can trust — someone who won't stomp me into the ground when I'm losing, when I'm going under! *(SPIDER WOMAN points— A beam of light comes up from the earth at his feet — TRICKSTER whirls away.)*

COYOTE: *(Fast)* Is it a question of acting natural? — not too forward, one step back, but not above it — when people say bad things about me, I don't get upset — it goes right by me — The respect of my peers! Fame and glory — I can get laid anytime I want to, and when Coyote's name is mentioned, people nod sagely and allow themselves a little smile! *(SPIDER WOMAN points— A light comes on in the earth. COYOTE whirls.)*

TRICKSTER: *(Fast)* The guilty party! — Psychoanalysis! — How my father stood by idly while my mother ruined my life! — Yes! It's not too late! — I can still win! — I can triumph! — I can make them pay through the nose! I can make it! *(SPIDER WOMAN points. A beam of light appears under TRICKSTER. There are now four beams of light shining out of the ground.)*

COYOTE: Wait! The double helix! The genetic code! Mutation! Power!

SPIDER WOMAN: Only Earthmaker knows the code.

TRICKSTER: *(Discouraged)* I guess that's it, then. No code. *(Enraged)* It's a trick! I will boil you in your kettle! I will make you into soup! I will send you back to your loony bin in a hundred thousand parts!

SPIDER WOMAN: *(Stopping him with a wave of her hand)* No. Try to concentrate your mind.

COYOTE: *(Distracted)* Why have all these lights come on in the earth?

SPIDER WOMAN: That is my power talking!

COYOTE: *(Admiring)* Great! *(The lights in the earth go out as SPIDER WOMAN sadly becomes HOMELESS CRAZY WOMAN again.)*

COYOTE AND TRICKSTER: Wait! Come back from the Homeless Crazy Woman and be Spider Woman again! Please!

SPIDER WOMAN: *(Giving them another chance)* Spider Woman is gone now, but she can speak through me. *(Listens)* She says, first, "How did white people come to be made on this earth?"

COYOTE: It was me who did it, and it wasn't easy. Outside Alamogordo the sand is only white — many people sitting on the ground, on the white sand. Then all at once they TURN. SNAP. And they put their hands up as a shield to the LIGHT — and they see through their hands. To the white bone shining. And they see the SOUND coming. And the sound is burning. *(Pause)* So I took this band of people and I put them in a box. I carried them into the mountains, to one of my high places, and I washed them in the snow until they were as white as the sand of Alamogordo. It wasn't easy.

Their skin was steaming. I burned my hands in the boiling snow. And they were bleeding. From the nose, from the ears, from the eyes, from the anus, from the sex organs. And the children also. It wasn't easy, but that is how white people came to be made on earth.

SPIDER WOMAN: *(Listening)* Spider Grandmother says, "Okay. I liked your story very much. But if you want an answer to your question, you have to ask it four times. If you can ask four times, it will mean that your mind is a little concentrated. But I warn you, you'd better be prepared for the consequences if something goes wrong. You might get stuck."

COYOTE AND TRICKSTER: I want to get back to my own tribe and see the real world!

SPIDER WOMAN: I tell you — try to understand what I say, or all the two-legged walking beings on earth, the five colors and five directions, all the people, born and unborn, now and forever, will have to work for a living!

COYOTE AND TRICKSTER: Don't worry!

SPIDER WOMAN: *(Listening)* And one more thing.

COYOTE AND TRICKSTER: Yes?

SPIDER WOMAN: You will have to pay for her advice.

COYOTE AND TRICKSTER : How much?

SPIDER WOMAN: *(Listens)* One blanket each.

COYOTE AND TRICKSTER: Oh.

SPIDER WOMAN: Now– Ask four times!

COYOTE AND TRICKSTER: How can I get back to my own world and see the real tribe? No...

COYOTE: How can I get back to my own blanket and see the real world?

TRICKSTER: No. How can I get back to my own world and see the real problem?

COYOTE: No. How can I get back to my own life and see the real tribe?

TRICKSTER: No. How can I get back to my own problems and live a real life?

COYOTE: Shut up! I almost had it!

TRICKSTER: WHAT?

COYOTE: How can I...?

TRICKSTER: How can I...?

COYOTE: RETURN!

TRICKSTER: NO!

COYOTE: How can I return my blanket and get a new one?

TRICKSTER: NO!

COYOTE: A refund!

TRICKSTER: I feel that we have gotten far away now and that the original experience has lost its meaning.

COYOTE: Get back!

TRICKSTER: Forever.

COYOTE: How can I get back...?

TRICKSTER: How can I get back to my own tribe and see the real world?

SPIDER WOMAN: *(Banging the kettle)* One! One! One!

TRICKSTER: One?

(They go on like this, getting the words mixed up, going off on tangents, telling stories, accusing each other, driving themselves into a frenzy. SPIDER WOMAN bangs her kettle and counts out each success. Finally, they startle themselves by inadvertantly and at last asking for the fourth time.)

SPIDER WOMAN: Four! Four! Four! *PENDEJOS!* This is what Spider Grandmother says: "Coyote/Trickster, if you want to get back to your own tribe and see the real world — you have to give up being crazy! You have to get out of your old skin and get into a new one!"

(Hurling curses, she strips them of their blankets and withdraws. COYOTE and TRICKSTER stand naked except for outlandish bathing suits. But they soon adjust to the new situation with macho bravado, addressing each other a la Gary Cooper and Robert Redford.)

COYOTE: You know, Mr. Smith, your salvation is not of this world.

TRICKSTER: Where is it then, Mr. Brown?

COYOTE: In the next world, Mr. Smith. Our people are probably having a nice life there, where their cells aren't burning in the climate.

TRICKSTER: Actually, I think the problem was my mother, who started me worrying at an early age.

COYOTE: Well, don't think about it now. Now is the time for exchanging blankets.

TRICKSTER: Blankets? But we gave our blankets to the Homeless Crazy Woman.

COYOTE: Don't you understand? Underneath one blanket is another, a second blanket.

TRICKSTER: Where is it?

COYOTE: It's our skins! Now we can exchange blankets and get out of our old skins and into a new one!

TRICKSTER: Oh.

COYOTE: And not only that, but one blanket equals one experience. That way, you also get to say an experience.

TRICKSTER: I see.

COYOTE: And that experience can be your Death Song!

TRICKSTER: Makes perfect sense!

(They race behind the saguaro, up left. TRICKSTER quickly takes off his shoes and re-enters, COYOTE following in his tracks.)

TRICKSTER: In my dream, the cloud upon which I walk is full of holes: one for every step I take. *(He arrives centerstage and turns downstage.)* A boat is weighing anchor off the continent. It has made no sound. There is no sign on it. Some of the inhabitants have turned against each other. Some are wading out into the water. Some are busy with masts and sails and a flag.

COYOTE:　　　　　Divine is sunlight
　　　　　　　　Divine is Earthmaker's tent
　　　　　　　　Divine is the Spider Lady's posture

(They stop, down center.)

TRICKSTER:　　　My name is Mudhead!
　　　　　　　　I am born of Earth!
　　　　　　　　My Father's name is Taiowa!
　　　　　　　　And I cannot die!

(He falls to his knees. COYOTE draws a circle around him with white sand.)

COYOTE:　　　　　Divine is thunder
　　　　　　　　Divine is lightning
　　　　　　　　Divine is Coyote's Journey
　　　　　　　　From beginning to end

TRICKSTER:　　　Once I was a newborn child
　　　　　　　　And Coyote/Trickster was my name.
　　　　　　　　I knew nothing,

And nothing had been named.
Then I was awakened.
"Now you have to learn about life,"
My mother said,
"Now you have to learn about Man."
I became a human being
And walked among the two-leggeds
I saw the new colors in the sky
I tasted the new flavors in the earth
It was not pleasant to me
It was not agreeable to me

(COYOTE takes a posture behind him. TRICKSTER paints a red line down the center of his own body, from the top of his head to his navel.)

TRICKSTER: My death song
                    Is:
                    SHUT YOUR STARS.

(CLOWN blows a shrill whistle as COYOTE "skins" TRICKSTER and holds the skin aloft in triumph. A pause before CLOWN rushes on stage and chases them off in a cloud of dust. She approaches the Audience and stutters.)

CLOWN: There are thousands of these Trickster/Coyotes! Their robes are everywhere!

(She starts off. A Drumbeat. CLOWN stops and points upstage. The gods appear, rising up slowly behind the ruins. They are — masked — COYOTE, MUDHEAD, and SPIDER WOMAN. To the slow cadence of the drum, they walk down toward the Audience.)

END

V: Listening to Old Nana

Legendary Apache Warrior Old Nana.

CLOWN, playing a harmonica, arrives to escort the Audience. As the people gather round her, she suddenly sniffs and makes a face. COYOTE and TRICKSTER, poorly disguised, are there also, trying unsuccessfullly to be anonymous. COYOTE'S face is painted half blue, half white. TRICKSTER'S face is half red, half white. They can't help but push their way noisily to the front of the crowd.

CLOWN: *(Signing)* Hey! I heard some people around here who want to get back to their own tribe and see the real world!

COYOTE AND TRICKSTER: *(Unable to restrain themselves)* You heard of some people around here who want to get back to their own tribe and see the real world? *(CLOWN nods emphatically)* Who told you about it?

CLOWN: *(Signing)* I heard about it.

COYOTE AND TRICKSTER: You heard about it? Where?

CLOWN: *(Signing)* On the radio.

COYOTE AND TRICKSTER: Radio?

CLOWN: *(Signing)* Don't worry about it.

COYOTE: Who's worried?

TRICKSTER: Not me!

CLOWN: *(Signing)* Let's go, then! *(They move a ways down toward the space, before COYOTE and TRICKSTER stop everybody)*

COYOTE AND TRICKSTER: Wait a minute!

CLOWN: *(Signing)* What's the matter?

COYOTE AND TRICKSTER: *(Backing off)* Nothing's the matter.

CLOWN: *(Signing, slyly)* What's a bear?

COYOTE: *(Can't stop himself)* What's a bear? A bear is a reincarnated criminal!

TRICKSTER: A bear is ugly buttocks! *(CLOWN points them out to the Audience, but COYOTE and TRICKSTER step aside, pretending that they never said anything.)*

CLOWN: *(Signing, to All.)* Come along with me!   I'll show you something really interesting! *(They move on.)*

COYOTE AND TRICKSTER: Wait a minute! *(CLOWN stops. COYOTE and TRICKSTER pretend ignorance.)*

CLOWN: *(Signing)* What's a sunbeam?

COYOTE AND TRICKSTER: A sunbeam is a spider web!

CLOWN: *(Makes knowing signs to the Audience. TRICKSTER translates.)* Hey, I'll show you how Mr. Coyote got that shit-eating grin on his face! One time, they say, Coyote's face was nearly normal, like other people!

COYOTE: Horse Feathers! Baloney! Salami! Nolo Contendre! Etc.

(CLOWN entices everyone over near a rock. There is a hat on the rock, and SPIDER WOMAN — dressed in Man's clothes as in III: Planet of the Spider People, appears behind it.)

COYOTE: *(To SPIDER WOMAN)* You look very familiar to me. Who do you suppose you are?

SPIDER WOMAN: I am the person who takes care of this rock.

COYOTE: Tell me about this rock.

SPIDER WOMAN: You just leave it alone. I know all about you. You think you're a pretty rough fellow, but you better have respect for this rock. It is a living rock.

COYOTE: That's silly talk. You don't know anything at all.

SPIDER WOMAN: Okay, but I have a wonderful bird under this hat here. He is black and yellow and red, and he knows everything in the world. Anything I want to know, I just ask him. He is worth a lot!

COYOTE: Can he tell you how to get money?

SPIDER WOMAN: Oh, yeah. He tells me that all the time.

COYOTE: Let us see him.

SPIDER WOMAN: No. He only talks to his owner.

COYOTE: Sell him to us then.

SPIDER WOMAN: No. He is worth too much. You couldn't afford him.

COYOTE: Look, we'll give you everything we have. *(He begs a meagre handful of coins from the Audience.)* Now, let me have that bird!

SPIDER WOMAN: Well, all right. But listen, I have owned this bird a long time and he likes me. You'd better let me get pretty far away before you reach under and get him, or he'll fly away after me.

COYOTE: Fine. That's the way it'll be then.

SPIDER WOMAN: You see that place over there? When you see me get over there with all these other people, then you can reach under and grab him.

COYOTE: Okay!

(CLOWN and SPIDER WOMAN bring the Audience closer to the set.)

SPIDER WOMAN: When you reach under there, grab him hard!... Okay, now!

COYOTE: *(Grabbing under the hat)* Aaaah! It's a turd! He tricked me! Mudhead, you come over here and buy this shit from me!

TRICKSTER: *(Laughing)* No, thanks!

CLOWN: *(Signing)* Let's move along now!

TRICKSTER: Wait a minute!

CLOWN: *(Signing)* Now, what?

TRICKSTER: Where are you taking us?

CLOWN: *(Signing)* It's sort of a house! You can see and hear everything in that house!

COYOTE AND TRICKSTER: You can see and hear everything in that house? *(Suspiciously)* What else?

CLOWN: *(Signing)* There's a beautiful woman in there!

COYOTE AND TRICKSTER: Let's go! *(They start off again, but COYOTE stops them.)*

COYOTE: Wait a minute!

CLOWN: *(Signing)* What's wrong?

COYOTE: One time, I was going around, and early in the morning I came to a house where a beautiful woman lived with her husband. Pretty soon the husband came out to go hunting, so I went right in there. The woman was making a fire. I said, "I'll help you to make that fire." We started heating up some rocks. I said, "Is this good?" She said, "Oh, yes. That's good." I said, "Is this good?" She said, "Yes. It's very good." We were ready to play knife and awl when the husband walks right back into the house. I should have killed that guy.

TRICKSTER: You should have killed that guy.

COYOTE: He made me start eating those hot rocks. "Is this good?" he said. "Oh yes," I said, "very good."

TRICKSTER: Coyote's face started to get a little funny.

COYOTE: I had to eat all those hot rocks.

TRICKSTER: His face has been funny every since. *(Paranoid)* I am talking about fruit!

COYOTE: *(Pointing away from the set)* Let's go THAT way!

CLOWN: *(Signing)* Don't worry! This woman doesn't have a husband!

COYOTE AND TRICKSTER: Oh! This woman doesn't have a husband! *(They look at each other.)*

COYOTE: Who's worried?

TRICKSTER: Not me!

CLOWN: Let's go then. *(They go on a ways. COYOTE stops them.)*

COYOTE: Maybe this woman is a sorcerer! She might steal our power! She could have bad medicine!

TRICKSTER: She could have strange diseases!

COYOTE: She might change herself into all kinds of weird animals and things!

COYOTE AND TRICKSTER: She could be a DI-YIN!

SPIDER WOMAN: *(To Audience)* A DI-YIN is Apache. It means a person who has certain powers. Geronimo was a DI-YIN for war.

TRICKSTER: *(Paranoid)* She is talking about fruit!

SPIDER WOMAN: You act like you don't know the difference between someone trying to help you and someone taking advantage. *(To Audience)* Come on!

COYOTE AND TRICKSTER: *(Trying to head them off)* NO! NO! NO! You can't go in there! That place belongs to me! It's mine! I found it first! I've been working on it a long time! It wasn't easy either! I have a big investment! I don't want you going into that house! It's for your own good! It's a Hunter Killer Satellite! You only want to hurt me! You only want to kill me! This house is sacred to Coyote/Trickster! *(They race off.)*

SPIDER WOMAN: *(To Audience)* Coyote was running around the Universe and he got bitten on the arm by a Black Hole. Now he's crazy with Black Hole Fever. Don't pay any attention to him.

COYOTE AND TRICKSTER: *(Off)* You'll be sorry!

(A steady drumbeat as the Audience follows CLOWN inside the set, which is at once symbolic of a signal-receiving station and an ancient ceremonial enclosure. Perched right and left on poles are the COYOTE and MUDHEAD masks. SPIDER WOMAN stands guard at the entrance. As the Audience are being seated, CLOWN waits on the platform in front of what appears to be a sort of primitive instrument panel, or altar, constructed of sticks and branches and logs, bits of string and ribbon, old bones, skulls, etc. The Audience settled, the drumbeat ceases and CLOWN, signing, calls for attention.)

SPIDER WOMAN: *(Translating quietly as CLOWN signs)* Listen to me... This story is about listening... Mr. Coyote don't know how to listen... He got no sense... Mr. Coyote has to die first, before he can learn how to listen... Old Nana will teach Coyote how to listen with his whole body... *(CLOWN quickly demonstrates the series of postures signifying "Listening with the whole body." Then the houselights suddenly dim and the masks light up. The masks speak.)*

MASKS: Clown, take your place!

(The mask lights go off. CLOWN makes a face and an obscene gesture toward them, then goes to her place down right of the platform. A pause. TRICKSTER tunnels into the space, left, talking to himself very fast. He is wearing only bathing trunks, his body painted half red, half white.)

TRICKSTER: I gotta-gotta-gotta-gotta-gotta-I-- *(Pause)* Gotta-gotta-gotta-gotta FIND — *(Pause)* Gotta-gotta-gotta-gotta find — I — *(Pause)* The PLUG! *(Seeing the Audience)* HUUU! *(Smells, listens)* I hope nobody's been confusing the wires around here. Got no business around here. Gotta-gotta-gotta stay outa my way. Outa my way — outa my way — outa my way! Mine-mine-mine! *(Stops. Listens.)* If Coyote comes around here we're all in trouble. Don't know how to listen. Got no sense. *(Pause)* I am talking about fruit! *(Pause)* Gotta-gotta-gotta PLUG THE OUTLET! *(He takes some jacks and stuff from his sack and plugs one into the ground. Listens. Silence. Looks around. Digs into his sack for a piece of paper, reads.)* Three hundred miles north of Apache Junction. *(Stares at the paper, puzzled. Scratches his head. A familiar howl, off.)* Oh, No!

(COYOTE comes running into the space. In bathing trunks. Painted half blue, half white. TRICKSTER tries to bury himself back into his tunnel.)

COYOTE: Oh, boy! This is some interesting place! I'm glad I found this place! *(TRICKSTER growls.)* This looks like my old satellite! I have been here before! This looks like my old place!

TRICKSTER: Get outa here, Coyote, or I'll rip your face off!

COYOTE: HUUU! *(Looks, listens)* Why, its old Buffalo Head! What are you doing in my listening station? *(TRICKSTER growls.)* But that's okay. It's very nice to see you.

TRICKSTER: *(Scrambling out of his hole)* What?! Are you kidding me — are you kidding me — are you kidding me? This is MY station. I'm gonna — I'm gonna — I'm gonna —

COYOTE: Whoa! I built this house! Me, Coyote! It took a very long time, too!

TRICKSTER: *(Suspiciously)* Why?

COYOTE: Why? Well, I had to dig holes. I had to find lumber. I had to fit the pieces all together. I—

TRICKSTER: No! I mean why did you build it?

COYOTE: Come on, Man. Why are you taking such a bad attitude?

TRICKSTER: You're not serious! You don't know how to listen, and you got no sense!

COYOTE: I am serious.

TRICKSTER: You're going to screw everything up again!

COYOTE: I am a very serious person.

TRICKSTER: You are a blue and white idiot! *(Gets busy with his sack of stuff)* I gotta-gotta-gotta-gotta! I gotta-gotta-gotta-gotta ignore this asshole! I gotta make contact, gotta find —

COYOTE: HUUU! *(TRICKSTER, startled, drops his sack.)* You know what? When I was going around gathering stuff for my, uh, house here, I came to a realization.

TRICKSTER: *(Stares at him. COYOTE waits.)* Tell us your realization, fuckhead!

COYOTE: Okay. I realized that I didn't have to be me, because I could just as easily be somebody else. I could be almost anybody. I could even be you.

TRICKSTER: Ha! You can't be me! Only I can be me!

COYOTE: I can be all the animals and all the plants and all the human beings. So why worry about being me? It's silly. *(Reclines)*

TRICKSTER: *(Near tears, to Audience)* One time Coyote said to me, "Trickster, if you want to be yourself, you have to keep your pelvis in the ground. There's just no way you can do it otherwise. You have to keep your pelvis in the ground." That was when he thought he was an Intergalactic Sage. So I put my pelvis in the ground. *(Pause)* It took me fifteen years to walk to the corner grocery store to buy a loaf of bread! Fifteen years!

COYOTE: Time well spent. Very educational.

TRICKSTER: When?!

COYOTE: See, YOU got no sense. YOU don't know how to listen and YOU got no sense.

TRICKSTER: I just gotta get in touch with Earth Mother. I just gotta. She sent me on a very important mission... So please don't interfere.

COYOTE: I know what we should do. We should set up radar. That's why I built this place. We'll set up radar and get some signals in here. I'll show you how it's done.

TRICKSTER: *(Has made a little hole in the ground. He shouts into it.)* Earth Mother! Earth Mother! *(Puts his ear to the hole)* I think I hear something... She's trying to talk to me...

COYOTE: *(Digs a little hole and puts his ear to it.)* Yeah. *(Sound of a waterfall)*

TRICKSTER: Yeah, what?

COYOTE: It's a waterfall.

TRICKSTER: A waterfall in the ground?

COYOTE: Sure.

TRICKSTER: *(Amazed)* It's wonderful!

COYOTE: Come on, I'll show you another really fine thing. *(Finds a long white stick)*

TRICKSTER: Yes?

COYOTE: This here is a memory stick. It's got lots of memories in it. You take this stick and plug it in, uh, here, and you get a memory back. I've been working on this piece of business for a long time now. *(He tries it. Nothing happens.)* You know what?

TRICKSTER: No.

COYOTE: The faster a man runs, the higher the sun rises.

TRICKSTER: Who told you that?

COYOTE: Old Nana. I can run faster than any other being. Me, Coyote! It is a very fine sensation. That's what keeps the sun rising!

TRICKSTER: Gimme that! *(He takes the memory stick and tries it somewhere else. This time it works.)*

VOICE OF OLD NANA: *(Off, miked)* When the world is about to end, there will be no water and no rain. That's how you will know. There will be maybe two or three springs left on all the earth. To these, people will come and fight over the water and kill each other. That's how people will end. After that, the world will be made over. And those who had been white will be Indian, and those who were Indian will be white.

TRICKSTER: *(Astonished)* Who was that?

COYOTE: That was Old Nana. I don't know how he knows all that. He had a power, I guess.

VOICE OF OLD NANA: But you people don't know how to listen, so you might as well forget about it. *(TRICKSTER starts hitting himself in the head.)*

COYOTE: Maybe he's only kidding. Don't worry about it.

TRICKSTER: Who's worried?

COYOTE: *(Inadvertantly touches two rocks together and gets a shock.)* Aaaaaah! There's a connection over here! *(He touches the two rocks together again and we hear a short section from the "How can I get back to my own tribe and see the real world" improvisation from Coyote IV: Other Side Camp.)*

TRICKSTER: Hey, who are these guys? Where are they coming from?

COYOTE: Ah, that's just bunch of low-level static, Man. *(He separates the rocks, breaking the connection.)*

TRICKSTER: Wait a minute! We're making progress around here now! We're making contact! *(He frantically tries to rig up wires and plugs, etc.)*

COYOTE: You ain't gonna hear anything that way, Buffalo Head. That's not the way to go. We got to use radar. Infra-red. Spectro-sofac-sofac-sofac-cracy!

TRICKSTER: Shut up! *(Suddenly he makes contact, almost jumping out of his skin.)* Aaaah!

VOICE OF SPIDER WOMAN: *(Off, miked)* Trickster! Trickster!

TRICKSTER: Yes?

VOICE OF SPIDER WOMAN: Use the prayer stick! It holds your highest thoughts!

TRICKSTER: What? *(He moves. The connection is broken.)* Talk to me! What's a prayer stick? Earth Mother! Talk to me!

COYOTE: I didn't hear nothin'.

TRICKSTER: Give me that memory stick! *(He tries a connection. It works.)*

VOICE OF OLD NANA: You say that because you learn from a book, that you can build all those big houses and talk with each other at any distance and do many wonderful things. Now, let me tell you what we think. You begin when you are little to work hard, and work until you are men in order to begin fresh work. You say that you work hard in order to work well. After you get to be men, then, you say, the labor of life commences; then you build the houses and ships and towns and everything. Then, after you have got them all, you die and leave them behind. Now, we call that slavery. You are slaves from the time when you begin to talk until you die; but we are free as air. We never work. Our wants are few and easily supplied. The river, the wood, and the plain yield all that we require, and we will not be slaves, nor will we send our children to your schools, where they only learn to become like yourselves.

TRICKSTER: Was that him again?

COYOTE: *(Sagely)* Yes, that was Old Nana again. We always get Old Nana in this station here. You can bet that two out of three times we'll get Old Nana around here. *(TRICKSTER tries to plug the memory stick somewhere else, tying a pair of head phones to it and putting them on. He gets SPIDER WOMAN.)*

VOICE OF SPIDER WOMAN: Old Nana was a great Apache warrior. Once, when he was over seventy, he took a hundred fighters off the reservation with him and went on a raid. He was seventy. *(Sound of many hoofbeats)* They rode and rode, raiding and killing. He went on a twenty five-hundred-mile blitz on horseback — down into Old Mexico, then up through Texas and across Arizona. Three armies were after him and they never got him. He just got tired of it and went home. He was a pisser, was Old Nana...

COYOTE: Now he is high up in the Spirit World, almost as high as Coyote.

TRICKSTER: But what does he advise?

VOICE OF OLD NANA: Always live in a rough place on the side of a hill.

(They ponder. Then COYOTE, with studied ease, begins trying to clean his nails with the memory stick.)

TRICKSTER: You seem to have a casual attitude toward a very serious situation. I would describe our current dilemma as a desperate one, and yet your approach is macho-cool. Take note, first of all, that we have no clothes. You cannot help but see, as well, that, out of sheer anxiety, our color has changed. We are no longer painted like other people.

COYOTE: I don't think it's anxiety at all. There is a perfectly apparent scientific reason. You are trying to attract red vibrations, and I am trying to attract blue vibrations.

TRICKSTER: I don't know about you, but I find my appalling ignorance and egotism to be a source of great shame to me in the face of our real circumstances. It would seem to be a matter of primary importance that we make and sustain contact with a higher authority. However, since you appear to know your way around here, I shall do as you do. If you are calm and collected, then I, too, will be calm and collected. If you pretend that you know what you are doing, then I, too, will pretend that I know what I am doing. And so on.

(A silence. TRICKSTER does as COYOTE does. Annoyed, COYOTE replaces the stick. Decides to try to pick up a beautiful woman in the Audience. TRICKSTER and CLOWN go along. COYOTE reclines with nonchalance. So does TRICKSTER. COYOTE turns a little wheel made of twigs and twine and suddenly the sound effect of a train going by. COYOTE and TRICKSTER, astounded, stand and wave. The train passes. The sound effect of fire engines comes roaring through. COYOTE and TRICKSTER hit the deck and cover their heads. The sirens pass. Then the sound of footsteps above, crossing from right to left. COYOTE and TRICKSTER look up in awe.)

COYOTE: Old Nana... *(The footsteps pass. Then the sounds of an arriving stagecoach. COYOTE and TRICKSTER jump to their feet.)*

TRICKSTER: I remember that stagecoach. There in that coach was the most beautiful damsel I had ever laid my eyes on. Long blonde hair, blue eyes, the prettiest smile you ever seen, a blue cotton dress, little parasol over her arm. As she was trying to get out of the coach, she lifted her dress up a little, like this... But of course she couldn't, because the roads were full of mud. And then, before I could say bip, you went over there and picked her up!

COYOTE: Are you still thinking about her?

TRICKSTER: Yes! We had made a vow to Earthmaker...!

(The stagecoach is gone. Suddenly the hooting of an owl. COYOTE and TRICKSTER transform into OWLS, as in Coyote I: Pointing.*)*

COYOTE: Is that your animal, the Owl?

TRICKSTER: When the Owl is heard, someone dies.

(Now the sound of an arrow flying and hitting its mark. TRICKSTER falls. Another arrow. COYOTE falls. Now the sound of a woman weeping. COYOTE stands. TRICKSTER becomes "Spirit of the Dead" as in Coyote II: the Shadow Ripens.*)*

TRICKSTER: Coyote listened for the voices. He looked all around, but nothing happened. Coyote sat there in the middle of the prairie. *(COYOTE sits, his head in his arms.)* He sat there all night, but the lodge didn't appear again. In the morning, he heard meadowlarks...

(As they sit sadly, the sound of someone whistling "My Darling Clementine." At the second chorus, the sound and light begin to fade.)

TRICKSTER: No!... No... Wait!... Don't go...!

(He retreives the memory stick and begins waving it up and down— a slide of the Apache warrior, OLD NANA, is projected magically upon it, as if appearing in air. COYOTE and TRICKSTER are thunderstruck.)

COYOTE: Oh! It's Old Nana!

TRICKSTER: Oh!

VOICE OF OLD NANA: Coyote/Trickster, I have message for you from Earthmaker.

COYOTE AND TRICKSTER: Old Nana, tell us the message from Earthmaker!

VOICE OF OLD NANA: First you have to die, Coyote/Trickster. That way, you can learn how to listen for a change. You can start all over again.

COYOTE AND TRICKSTER: Die? But Old Nana....

VOICE OF OLD NANA: Don't worry about it.

COYOTE: Who's worried?

TRICKSTER: Not me! *(They stay put.)*

VOICE OF OLD NANA: Well, go ahead and die, then. *(COYOTE and TRICKSTER exchange looks, each waiting for the other to move first.)* Come on.

COYOTE: Go ahead.

TRICKSTER: No. You go.

COYOTE: After you.

TRICKSTER: I'm busy.

VOICE OF OLD NANA: Coyote, you hang yourself. Trickster, you bury your pelvis in the ground.

(The image of Old Nana disappears. TRICKSTER replaces the stick. They take a posture of homage. CLOWN plays a melody on a toy xylophone as COYOTE hangs himself from a crossbeam and TRICKSTER, below him, buries his pelvis in the ground.)

VOICE OF OLD NANA: Okay. Now you can say your death visions.

COYOTE: I see blue. I see human beings swimming around in a thick blue sea. They are gluing together and ungluing, gluing and ungluing. Mouth and member, mouth and organ, knife and awl. They're spreading germs all over the place. It's all very wet there. Wet and blue. All the organisms are swimming and gluing. The germs, too. They don't have time for anything else. If they're not doing it, they're thinking about it. But there are plenty of bodies. Enough to go around. Then they drown in the blue sea and nothing is left, not even a memory.

TRICKSTER: I see red. I see red beaches. I see people on the red beaches. Right at this moment I see millions of people on red beaches. Beautiful people! They're having a good time in the red sun. A few miles away, other people are getting bombed by flying machines. These beautiful people used to be reptiles, but they forgot about it. They don't pay any attention to the noise of the flying machines, and they don't know I'm seeing them now, oiling their bodies, shading their eyes from the red sun. They've got life all figured out. They don't know I am seeing them now! Isn't that remarkable?

COYOTE AND TRICKSTER: There they are on the red beaches thinking of the next thing while the blue oceans of that planet are crying a terrible death song. The oceans are singing their death songs. The flying machines pass over them in the sky — eagles shining in the red sun, with long white tails curling behind them. They are called — "Shine/Shine."

VOICE OF OLD NANA: Yeah. Alright. (Pause) The trouble with white people is they don't know how to die. There's no silence in their lives. They take it all personally and make a big deal out of it. (Pause) Let me tell you about tobacco. You people don't smoke right. Tobacco means earth, wind, fire. It comes into the lungs saying, "Ah, here am I." (Pause) Okay, now that you're dead, I can teach you how to listen. So, get ready. (COYOTE and TRICKSTER get ready.) First, the feet. Right foot.

(COYOTE, TRICKSTER and CLOWN, in her place, take the right foot posture.)

TRICKSTER: Right foot — listening — a story in the ground — a big wind came from far away and hit all the mountains — hard — it slowed the movement of the earth — everything on the earth shifted — the land where once was water, the water where once was land — all the animals from the land had to learn to live in the water — all the animals in the water had to learn to live on the land — and those that couldn't change — they died —

VOICE OF OLD NANA: Left foot.

(They take the left foot posture.)

COYOTE: Left foot — listening — a great silence — everything had to stand still — and out of the stillness came a light — and out of the light, two brothers singing — they sing while the small worlds die, crushed into nothing — these brothers love it — they want everything to be different — they're not happy with the way things are —

VOICE OF OLD NANA: Left knee.

(They take the left knee posture.)

TRICKSTER: Left knee — listening — too far above the ground — the music of a past culture — machines carrying things, creatures that aren't here anymore — loads of things moving from here to there — buzzing and moving —

VOICE OF OLD NANA: Right knee.

(They take the right knee posture.)

COYOTE: Right knee — listening — the wind whistles as I run — grabs my bone and lifts it in the air — I hear the fur growing and there are rabbits in the grass — hearts beating very fast — eyes turning — necks locking — ears too long — they are afraid of Coyote —

VOICE OF OLD NANA: Pelvis.

(They take the pelvis posture.)

TRICKSTER: Pelvis — listening — warm mother — warm enveloping mother in the ground — water flowing — head flying way above — moaning — sighing —

COYOTE: Pelvis — listening — someone making music on the top of the hills — it is making my pelvis vibrate — my pelvis holds my penis — perfectly —

VOICE OF OLD NANA: Stomach.

(They take the stomach posture.)

COYOTE: Stomach — listening — jet engine vibrating — all the trees in the world sigh — all the trees in the world —

TRICKSTER: Stomach — listening — the wind blowing through — my stomach hears the wind blowing through —

VOICE OF OLD NANA: Solar plexus.

(They take the solar plexus posture.)

TRICKSTER: Solar plexus — listening — Spider Grandmother is walking over huge rocks — she's looking for a hole to take a shit in — whoops, she's upside down — whoops, this could be dangerous — she doesn't care — here's a big green rock she can see right through — but she walks past it — she doesn't care —

VOICE OF OLD NANA: Heart.

(They take the heart posture.)

COYOTE: Heart — listening — the buffalo are dying — bellowing — they're all in mud — they're groaning — Trickster is sitting on one — naked, riding, painted red and white — the buffalo bellows — it falls — Trickster falls — he is stuck in the mud, bellowing — it is time to leave this place —

VOICE OF OLD NANA: Right arm.

(They take the right arm posture.)

COYOTE: Right arm — listening — children dying — they are bleeding —

VOICE OF OLD NANA: Left arm.

(They take the left arm posture.)

TRICKSTER: Left arm — listening — from the nose — from the mouth — from the eyes — from the anus — from the sex organs —

VOICE OF OLD NANA: Back.

(They take the back posture.)

TRICKSTER: Back — listening — it doesn't have a skin — lost buffalo robe hump — electricity — whips — flies — millions of dead fish — someone took its blanket —

VOICE OF OLD NANA: Spine.

(They take the spine posture.)

COYOTE: Spine — listening — she had legs like wings — she had eyes like stones in a stream — she had arms like trees — she had hair like corn — she had feet like birds — she had hands like flowers — she had a mouth like —

VOICE OF OLD NANA: Right face.

(They take the right side of the face posture.)

COYOTE: Right face — listening — giant ants marching in an endless row — they want to come into my head — through the eyes — through the nose — through the ears — they want to come in — my forehead falls ten thousand feet down into my mouth —

VOICE OF OLD NANA: Left face.

(They take the left side of the face posture.)

TRICKSTER: Left face — listening — oh! Hurts and losses and sharp stones and ice and kisses and so many things — more than all the stars in the sky —

VOICE OF OLD NANA: Skull.

(They take the skull posture.)

TRICKSTER: Oh! — the singing of insects — so many insects my head can't hold them all! — Oh! There is a very large wasp on its way now!

COYOTE: Oh! — it's my planet! — everyone lives there in my planet! — It's very clean! — everyone is doing their job — they work in little polished caves!

COYOTE AND TRICKSTER: While the insects are singing to them! *(They perform the "Singing of the Insects," concluding:)* Huuu!

VOICE OF OLD NANA: *(Harsh whisper)* Coyote/Trickster. This is the message from Earthmaker... the Hard Punishment is coming.

COYOTE AND TRICKSTER: Huuu!

(Very slow dim out as they do the "Singing of the Insects" five times, acknowledging the five directions. The masks light up in the darkness. COYOTE/TRICKSTER is gone.)

(The masks continue the "Singing of the Insects" four times as CLOWN takes an attitude of terror and supplication with her into the Audience.)

THE MASKS: Huuu!

(Blackout.)

END

VI: THE SACRED DUMP

COYOTE (Darrell Larson), left, is in the "right knee" listening posture, while TRICKSTER (Norbert Weisser), wearing his Buffalo headdress, holds the "pelvis" listening posture, on *The Sacred Dump* set.

COYOTE listens to TRICKSTER as Coyote's father and SPIDER WOMAN (Christine Avila) as the Gargoyle in *The Sacred Dump*.

THE SCENE: Some twenty-five yards wide by seventy yards deep of open space. Extreme upstage right is a kind of ramp which has no useful function and reminds us of nothing. COYOTE makes his entrance on it. Up left is a round object which could be a meteorite — the "planet." There are other objects — as well as sources of light — that look like nothing we've ever seen. Poles fifty feet high, holes in the ground, fissures. Center stage, about thirty yards from the Audience, is the Germ God, some six feet in diamater and twelve feet high. Down right from the Germ God is what appears to be the carcass of an American Buffalo. Down left from the Germ God, about ten yards up from the Audience, is SPIDER WOMAN's spot high in a tree or tree-like structure. She is in the center of an enormous web, the lines of which extend in every direction.

A strange sound in the space, reminiscent of the "The Singing of Insects" in Coyote V: Listening *to Old Nana. A long wait as the sound builds in intensity and volume. It is interrupted suddenly by the eerie, chilling, and yet poignant cry of a huge wounded ant, whom we do not see. The sound of the insects begins to fade, and then, gradually, SPIDER WOMAN's face appears high up in her perch:*

SPIDER WOMAN: I am Gogyeng Sowuuti! *(She smiles.)* Some of you I know by your names! Some I know by — your actions! Others I know by your thoughts! But all of you I know by your nature! *(Fiercely)* It was me who brought you here to this place! ME! *(Smiles)* You can come out now, child! *(Pause. Gently)* Come out!

(CLOWN appears from within the Germ God.)

SPIDER WOMAN: Come down!

(CLOWN races downstage to the Audience.)

SPIDER WOMAN: Remember, child, my instructions to you concerning the Fourth World?

(CLOWN mischieviously shakes her head "No.")

SPIDER WOMAN: It was not all beautiful and easy like the previous ones. It had height and depth, heat and cold, beauty and barrenness.

(CLOWN shakes her head "Yes.")

SPIDER WOMAN: What was this world called?

CLOWN: *(Half-signing)* World com-pete!

SPIDER WOMAN: Good! World complete! It had everything to choose from! But it was up to the people to help carry out the Plan of Creation!

CLOWN: *(Half-signing)* There are no song birds here! There are no little creatures who mean no harm!

SPIDER WOMAN: There are no song birds here. There are no little creatures who mean no harm. Things are very abnormal here. *(Sighs)* I'll tell you what happened– the Third World failed. It was flooded. I had to save the people who were not yet shifty-eyed, sly, cynical, lying sonsofbitches! It was ME who saved them!

CLOWN: I know that already! I know all that already!

SPIDER WOMAN: Oh, so you know that already. Well, then talk!

CLOWN AND SPIDER WOMAN: *(CLOWN half-signs)* The people forgot why they were here and that Taiowa was their father! We had to move to a higher world! The sun turned red! The air got thick! The earth cracked! The buildings fell down! We heard footsteps in the sky! *(CLOWN is trying to act all this out.)* We thought we could escape up there through a hole in the sky. We'll build a bamboo ladder and send a bird up there to talk to whoever is walking around up there. A bird climbed up and flew though the hole in the sky — and came back! He spoke to Massauwu, God of the Dead, who lives on the other side! He says — it's okay! We can come up there and live! But we have to try and be — real human beings! The Fire Clan goes up first and reaches the hole in the sky! The other clans follow! But there are Evil Ones among us! We kick down the ladder, so no more can come up! We are in the Fourth World! *(Pause)*

CLOWN: The Fourth World! The Fourth World! Come on — I have a job to do here!

SPIDER WOMAN: Hold your horses! I know you have a job to do! I gave it to you! So, in the Fourth World, they went to Massauwu and asked him to be their leader. "No thanks," he says, "You go your way and I'll go mine." *(Laughs)* He came over to me one time while we were resting on one of the rungs of the Solar System. "Gogyeng Sowuuti," he said to me, "I know you are working for Earth Mother, and have to do your job, but those people you saved, they are carrying bad germs in them." "What germs?" I asked him. "The germ of fear; the germ of greed; the germ of too much thinking. They'll forget why they are alive and try to have power over the Spirit. They won't be able to see reality. You'll have plenty trouble. This world will be poisoned, and the Spirit withdrawn." He knew what he was talking about. He advised me to keep on friendly terms with the Germ God, Muyingwa.

CLOWN: He's my friend!

SPIDER WOMAN: It's true. He likes you very much. *(CLOWN beams)* He'll come in handy later, when we start all over again with a new Code. *(Laughs)* The Fourth World, the World Complete, was punished and destroyed.

CLOWN: *(Of the Audience)* Are there strange creatures in this place?

SPIDER WOMAN: Yes, but don't be afraid. They're only imaginary creatures now. They're ghosts. They're not real anymore. They just imagine each other being there.

CLOWN: What happens when they die?

SPIDER WOMAN: When they die, they don't join the Spirit World; they go into crevices in the ground and become poisonous gases.

CLOWN: Ugh!

SPIDER WOMAN: You see, Child, it's a very interesting thing. The Fourth World looks like it's still there. *(Laughs)* Intact. They don't realize that the Spirit has been taken out of it.

CLOWN: What can we do?

SPIDER WOMAN: Do? Wait, I'll come down!

CLOWN: Oh!

SPIDER WOMAN: *(Chanting, as she makes her spidery descent)* Oh! Many stones! Many people together! They stored their goods and armed themselves! Water in the canyons! Oh! The cities! The towns! The great Kivas! The fire signals! The shine/shine! The screaming of the Cloud People! *(She hits the ground, taking the Warrior's posture)* Huuuu! I, Gogyeng Sowuuti, saw and heard these things!

(Now, as she speaks the following, she takes the series of postures indicated by OLD NANA in Coyote V.)

SPIDER WOMAN: The people thought they had it all coming to them, just because they happened to get born. They didn't listen to their good spirits. The water was poisoned. The air was poisoned. The earth was poisoned. And when the Hard Punishment came — some tried to escape through a hole in the sky! They didn't make it. They fell into everlasting silence. One of those was... Coyote! Some tried to escape through a hole in the ground! They didn't make it. They got burned alive! And one of those was... Trickster! Many others! They locked themselves up! They crawled into cellars and burrows and rooms! It was each one for himself! None of them made it either. They had become — DERANGED INSECTS!

(SPIDER WOMAN and CLOWN scream "The Singing of the Insects" keening sound from Coyote V, CLOWN taking a posture of supplication... SPIDER WOMAN stops and goes to her)

SPIDER WOMAN: *(Gently)* Don't worry, they're all part of the chemical soup now. *(Laughs)* While you... you're here with me.

CLOWN: I think someone else is around here too!

SPIDER WOMAN: Right! Coyote/Trickster is around here! I just experienced his presence. Now we have to call him out as a witness.

CLOWN: They won't come out! They're scared!

SPIDER WOMAN: I know they're scared.

CLOWN: They won't come out!

SPIDER WOMAN: They'll come out if we arouse their curiosity. The one thing they can't resist is women and curiosity... We'll make a big hullabaloo.

CLOWN: *(Half-signing)* Boo!

SPIDER WOMAN: Hullabaloo.

CLOWN: Boo!

SPIDER WOMAN: Say it. Hullababoo. Never mind. This is what you do—you hand these instruments out to some of these imaginary kids here. Then, when I give you the signal, start those kids waving them in the air. Then Coyote/Trickster will come out.

CLOWN: *(Hands out the instruments to kids in the Audience.)* Okay!

SPIDER WOMAN: Wait! I have to get back up my tree! If they see me here, they won't come out!

CLOWN: Right! *(SPIDER WOMAN climbs back into her tree.)*

SPIDER WOMAN: Okay! Start... Now!

(CLOWN conducts the kids waving the instruments. The sound is like the humming of strange insects. A few beats, then COYOTE howls, off. CLOWN intensifies her efforts. Another howl, and a groan from TRICKSTER. TRICKSTER is down right, in the body of the dead buffalo. COYOTE scampers out onto the ramp up right, stops, howls. CLOWN chases the kids back into the Audience. TRICKSTER groans and stands, shaking off the buffalo, but keeping his headdress. COYOTE leaps from the ramp, bounding high into the air. They move about the space, quickly taking the series of postures given them by OLD NANA in Coyote V, until finally meeting each other in front of the Germ God.)

COYOTE: Buffalo-Head!

(He scampers to TRICKSTER and hugs him. TRICKSTER, confused, decides too late to respond. Now both are embarrassed. COYOTE retreats.)

TRICKSTER: Coyote!

(Suddenly they become aware of themselves in the strange environment and

are stunned, frozen to the spot. They look fearfully around. They look at the Audience. They look at each other again. They try to run — but CLOWN knocks on her wooden block, holding them in place.)

FIRST EXCHANGE

SPIDER WOMAN: Coyote — you need something?

COYOTE: Yes. I need to give my pain room to stretch...

TRICKSTER: I didn't have a bag for it. You need the right vessel. Like a net that you could hold it in, or a bag. A vessel...

COYOTE: Pain is the vessel, and you hold on to it in order to float...?

(They try to run, but CLOWN knocks.)

SECOND EXCHANGE

SPIDER WOMAN: Tell us one thing that happens a lot.

COYOTE AND TRICKSTER: I hang myself up in an embarrassing situation, and then later I say...

COYOTE: I did that on purpose, for the other person's benefit.

TRICKSTER: No way you can get caught, you tell yourself shit like that.

(They try to run— CLOWN knocks.)

THIRD EXCHANGE

SPIDER WOMAN: What were you doing out there?

COYOTE: I was looking for a woman who had no problems! I never found one!

SPIDER WOMAN: That's not enough.

TRICKSTER: I was dancing. I was dancing. I was dancing. That's what I was doing. Dancing. Something disturbed me. Dancing. I don't remember. Something disturbed me. Small. Like a fly. I shoulda just stomped on it. Squashed it. It was nothing! Nothing!

(He flings away his headdress in disgust. They try to run. CLOWN knocks.)

FOURTH EXCHANGE

SPIDER WOMAN: What did you have?

COYOTE: We always had someone to dance with.

TRICKSTER: You could never step without stumbling!

COYOTE: We always had quarters for the juke box.

TRICKSTER: You could never fly without falling!

COYOTE: We always had cups of coffee.

TRICKSTER: You could never fart without hurting!

COYOTE: We always had clean sheets on our beds.

TRICKSTER: You could never eat without ripping your throat!

COYOTE: We always had great sex.

TRICKSTER: You could never have sex without catching a disease!

COYOTE: The maitre d' always seated you.

TRICKSTER: You could never laugh without crying!

COYOTE: We always had plenty tears.

TRICKSTER: You could never swim without drowning! It was a hell of a place! *(Pause)*

COYOTE: I have nothing. *(Pause)*

(Again they try to run — CLOWN knocks.)

FIFTH EXCHANGE

SPIDER WOMAN: Where were you going?

COYOTE: I was on my way. I forgot where I was going. I forgot why. I forgot my starting point. I couldn't remember. I was lost.

TRICKSTER: How could this be happening? How could this be happening to me?

COYOTE: It doesn't matter. It doesn't matter which way I go. I could go THIS way.

TRICKSTER: I could go THAT way.

COYOTE: It doesn't matter. I could keep right on going. *(Pause)* The Fourth World is round.

(They try to run — CLOWN knocks.)

SIXTH EXCHANGE

SPIDER WOMAN: What was there?

TRICKSTER: There used to be a mountain, and another mountain, and trees, and birds singing, and a bunch of cars in the parking lot. *(Pause)* And then there was a light. And fog came down on the mountain. *(Pause)* Then it all went away.

(They try to run for the last time — CLOWN knocks.)

SEVENTH EXCHANGE

COYOTE: Everybody knows how to run. Everyone knows how to feel sorry.

(CLOWN spits. TRICKSTER becomes entranced with the spit.).

COYOTE: Animals know when it's cold. That's all I know. There-fore, I am an animal. *(CLOWN knocks)* It's like we're all out on the street. *(Pause)* I thought everything was all right... but the sidewalk blew up.

(CLOWN knocks.)

EIGHTH EXCHANGE

SPIDER WOMAN: What comes here?

TRICKSTER: *(Waking)* The lost moments come here. This is where we keep them. That's why it glows. *(Pause)* We don't really bring THAT moment here, we bring THIS moment here.

COYOTE: My father sits all alone in a room.

(CLOWN strikes the bell.)

NINTH EXCHANGE

SPIDER WOMAN: What happened to the Fourth World?

COYOTE: We had to get out!

TRICKSTER: We were all huddled!

COYOTE: Strangers grabbed my tail!

TRICKSTER: In a creek bed! But we couldn't breathe!

COYOTE: I had to lead them out!

TRICKSTER: Licking our wounds!

COYOTE: I had to jump very high!

TRICKSTER: Then the rain came! Felt like hot fire coming down! Burning our coats! Stinking flesh, rotting bones!

COYOTE: Insects!

TRICKSTER: Stinking flesh!

COYOTE: I'll kill them all!

TRICKSTER I'm not through yet! I've got plans! We few survivors!

COYOTE: I smelled it coming!

TRICKSTER: Walk our squashed bones! Our empty eye-sockets!

COYOTE: They grabbed my tail!

TRICKSTER: I was a little bee, dying, covered with dust...

COYOTE: I threw a rope through the hole in the sky!

TRICKSTER: There was talking, then everything stopped. And then I remembered.

COYOTE: Then the rope broke and they tumbled down!

TRICKSTER: And then I forgot.

COYOTE: Like rain.

(CLOWN knocks.)

TENTH EXCHANGE

TRICKSTER: There's a big hole in the ground that I know. You can travel through it to the center of the Earth, but you have no control over where you're going. It just swallows you — like a seed, like a germ.

ELEVENTH EXCHANGE

COYOTE: One day I will learn how to roll my own cigarettes. In the meantime, I have to smoke Lucky Strikes, and smoke every single one of them very fast. *(To TRICKSTER)* This morning I was on a planet all alone, a perfectly smooth copper planet. I could run around it in less that ten minutes. And there are no flies there.

SPIDER WOMAN: That's not enough.

TRICKSTER I don't want to talk anymore! *(CLOWN knocks.)* As I think it, it turns into nothing! *(CLOWN knocks.)* I have to learn how to speak faster than I think! *(CLOWN knocks.)* I have to learn to speak as I think! *(CLOWN knocks.)* I have to learn how to speak!

(CLOWN knocks.)

TWELFTH EXCHANGE

SPIDER WOMAN: And before thought?

COYOTE: Before I became a human being, I, Coyote, was all creatures. First-born I was!

TRICKSTER: Everything around me was trying to eat me. Everything around me is trying to eat me to this day!

COYOTE: It was all in the seed of my Father, Taiowa, and I evolved into something really fantastic — I could fly!

TRICKSTER: I was an eating machine, like all the others —

COYOTE: At first I could only glide... And then I lost weight... And then I... I could fish! I could dive into the water, to the bottom, for food!

TRICKSTER: Feathers need careful maintenance! Jays and crows are particularly addicted to angry ants — they eat the other insects!

COYOTE: My arms had a feeling of lightness. My heart was empty and my belly was full. My head was a pair of eyes. I could see the inside of things by their nature, by their powers and colors!

TRICKSTER: A reptile, hitting the ground, avoiding a stall and a crash, its wings beating the heavy air...!

COYOTE: It's a simple question of flight control. Oh! I had a beak that could suck nectar!

TRICKSTER: Everything is alive! When it gets murdered, it stinks! I knew all these odors by their nature, by their powers and flavors!

(CLOWN gets the kids to start waving their instruments again, accompanying COYOTE/TRICKSTER's frenzy, and using her own instrument to help sustain and build it, moves behind them upstage center and pushes them downstage toward the Audience.)

COYOTE: I sing my song! It penetrates all thickets! And not only that —I will mate with my own! So all you rivals, you better answer me!

TRICKSTER: I rutted! I was in heat! I would fuck anything that moved!

COYOTE: I am a fine thing! I display myself! I am spectacular! I am a bird of paradise!

TRICKSTER: My wife's friends, my friends' wives, my daughters, my daughter's friends, my sisters, my sisters' friends, the beasts in the field and their shepherds! *(Stops and bellows like a buffalo in heat.)*

COYOTE: My life is devoted to dancing! I am Coyote! All creatures of paradise, I am them all! I must be beautiful! And here is the climax of my performance! *(He is all puffed up.)*

(CLOWN stops the music. TRICKSTER cums and is exhausted. An awkward silence. COYOTE and TRICKSTER subside.)

THIRTEENTH EXCHANGE

SPIDER WOMAN: And now?

(COYOTE walks away. TRICKSTER tries to recover his poise.)

TRICKSTER: There's a very thin line drawn from that point to here. And you try to keep it, but it gets thinner as you come down... it stays there...

COYOTE: Once it's happened, it's gone. It doesn't matter where you look. You have to look up, you have to look down. Once it's happened, it's gone.

TRICKSTER: You're connected, very thin, thinning out into just between my fingers, like so...

COYOTE: While it's happening, it's gone. Happening is gone.

TRICKSTER: You can't really trust your left side. It always wants to add something.

COYOTE: It happens to everyone. All we have is what we remember. We do what we know how to do. All we know how to do is die.

(CLOWN knocks.)

FOURTEENTH EXCHANGE

SPIDER WOMAN: How are you?

(They hesitate. CLOWN knocks.)

TRICKSTER: I'm talking and it don't sound right. I'm saying things for no reason. I don't mean it. I'm just saying things. It comes out harshly. Then I fall silent, stiff. I'm dead. People are embarrassed. They think I'm strange. Then someone makes a joke. I laugh like a corpse. Ha ha ha.

(CLOWN knocks.)

COYOTE: I'm very sorry. I surrender... I'm very ashamed. I meant it, but I'm still ashamed.

TRICKSTER: I don't talk right. The owls and the crows talk better than me. The sparrows talk better than me.

COYOTE: When I became a human being, I fell out of the womb of a woman. I had been implanted there. I fell out of a hole in the sky into the body of a woman, like a seed. I was an egg in the body of a woman. This woman, my mother, was also once an egg/seed. This was the beginning of a transformation — from egg/seed, to female, to grotesque. It had all been prepared, in time, by the poison in the shell of the seed.

TRICKSTER: I don't walk right. The beetles walk better than me, the four-leggeds walk better than me. The wounded dogs walk better than me!

COYOTE: When I was a child everything was familiar to me and had power. The air had power, the earth had power, the sky had power. The power was the Spirit in all things and I knew it personally — me, Coyote!

(CLOWN knocks.)

FIFTEENTH EXCHANGE

SPIDER WOMAN: And then?

(COYOTE tries to speak, cannot.)

SPIDER WOMAN: And then?

COYOTE: In the twilight of the Fourth World, Taiowa withdrew the Spirit. I was on my own.

SIXTEENTH EXCHANGE

SPIDER WOMAN: What are you?

COYOTE AND TRICKSTER: I am the living tip of the long line of the dead, like the head of a worm, the long line of the dead...

(CLOWN knocks. TRICKSTER sits at the foot of SPIDER WOMAN's tree. COYOTE kneels.)

SEVENTEENTH EXCHANGE

SPIDER WOMAN: Who brought you?

COYOTE: My father.

TRICKSTER: *(As COYOTE's father)* Coyote?

COYOTE: Hi, Dad.

TRICKSTER: You look the same.

COYOTE: You look the same.

TRICKSTER: You know what's happening to me?

COYOTE: Yes.

TRICKSTER: Yeah... They all come to me now. Now they all come. It's very dramatic.

COYOTE: Me, too. I've come, too.

TRICKSTER: I got it coming to me. People, money, whatever. I got it now.

COYOTE: You got it.

TRICKSTER: Your sisters and brothers, your aunts and uncles, they're all coming to see me now.

COYOTE: What else?

TRICKSTER: I took care of my car. It's in the shop this minute. It's a Caddie. Right front tire bald on one side. Alignment's off. An imperfection. I'm taking care of it. Pay the man later, if he'll wait. (Pause) I got the right number for you, finally?

COYOTE: What number?

TRICKSTER: 396-9216. Area code 213.

COYOTE: That's it.

TRICKSTER: Same number? That's the number?

COYOTE: That's my number.

TRICKSTER: That's the one I have!

COYOTE: You've had the right number.

TRICKSTER: Holy shit.! All these years!

COYOTE: That's the number.

TRICKSTER: I thought you moved!

COYOTE: That's the number. So, how you doin'?

TRICKSTER: Well, you know. I'll be goin' to work.

COYOTE: Will you? That's great.

TRICKSTER: Oh, yeah! Sure! They can't do it without me. Run the show. I'm the one knows the machines. Sound and all. Especially the sound. Do that myself. Oh, yeah.

COYOTE: What happened?

TRICKSTER: One day I shit out my bowels. Stool covered with blood. Large intestine came out. Colon came out. Oh, yeah. Now they say it's in my liver. Oh, yeah. Big discussion. Your aunts and uncles. Your brothers and sisters. Chemotherapy. Oh, yeah, sure. We'll see. Makes you sick and your hair falls out. (Pause, looking off) Did you see that?

COYOTE: What?

TRICKSTER: It rained! It rained for the flutter of an eye! Did you catch it? It was a fantasy! (Laughs) Oh, yeah!

(CLOWN strikes the bell. COYOTE rises.)

COYOTE: I walked down to the road. Once I had been child in this place. The world was shining in a bright light. There was the road.

(CLOWN knocks. COYOTE starts walking away.)

EIGHTEENTH EXCHANGE

SPIDER WOMAN: Who gave you life? (COYOTE keeps walking.) Who gave you life?

(CLOWN strikes the bell. COYOTE stops.)

COYOTE: My mother. It was her mother who created her — and so on, back to the beginning, the long worm of the dead. She, my Grandmother, created my mother... a gargoyle. (He looks up into the tree where SPIDER WOMAN has become the GARGOYLE.) It wasn't easy. First with violence, then with coldness, and then with crazy indifference. And then she was ready. My mother was ready.

TRICKSTER: She never rolled over and put out! She never gave! Your mother had nothing to give but vengeance! She was already dead! *(Pause)* And me? Your father?

COYOTE: *(To TRICKSTER)* She beat me at dawn and she beat me at twilight.

TRICKSTER: So what?

COYOTE: She used a coal shovel.

TRICKSTER: Big deal!

COYOTE: *(To Audience)* She was trying to beat the strength out of Coyote, but she was making him mad at the same time. *(Pause)* This was in the twilight of the Fourth World.

TRICKSTER: And me? I was dead, too. Finished. I would fuck anything that moved. Anything female. I suppose the animal was alive. *(Pause)* She never put her arms around me with affection. She never eased my way. No help. And she was unclean. Unclean. I'd kill her, but what would be the point?

COYOTE: I took the coal shovel from her hands. I said, "You do that again, and I'll kill you." She never did it again. I was on my own. Time passed. She could no longer function. They had to put her away.

SPIDER WOMAN: *(As COYOTE's mother)* Coyote, don't sign the papers! Don't let them give me treatments! Your father wants to kill me!

TRICKSTER: I couldn't sign the papers. I was illegal myself. Incompetent, a jailbird! *(Shrieks as CROW)* An animal! *(Pause)* They never asked me about it! They ganged up on me! They were out to get me! They put me in prison! They wouldn't take MY word for it! They took everybody else's word but mine!

COYOTE: I went on a long journey and I signed the papers. They gave her shocks. *(The tree shakes.)* And again. *(The tree shakes.)* And again. *(The tree shakes.)* They calmed her down. I felt guilty. They said it was all for the best. But she had been the source of terrific pain... And she taught me the alphabet, in English, when I was small.

SPIDER WOMAN: I'm already dead. All three of my natures. Dead, almost from the beginning. Now I chew my pills, my chemical cud. Time passes. The government takes care of me. They owe me, for all I have suffered. The failures of men.

COYOTE: The Gargoyle was completed.

SPIDER WOMAN: Ah. Ah.

NINETEENTH EXCHANGE

TRICKSTER: *(Standing, as though seeing)* There are strange creatures in the dark, under the sea.

COYOTE: No one is going anywhere. No one is coming from anywhere.

TRICKSTER: They don't use oxygen, these creatures.

COYOTE: Everything has already happened.

TRICKSTER: They are like worms.

COYOTE: All I see is movement. Nothing else is happening.

TRICKSTER: They eat sulphur. They breathe nitrogen.

COYOTE: It's a diagram!

TRICKSTER: They live near the fire in the center of the Earth.

COYOTE: I am nothing at all!

TRICKSTER: Earthmother is making life under the sea, in the dark...

(The ANT cries out, off. TRICKSTER takes his protective posture. The ANT cries again. TRICKSTER looks off into the darkness.)

SPIDER WOMAN: There is a wounded insect around here. She is hurt bad. She needs help.

TRICKSTER: Yeah?

SPIDER WOMAN: Yeah. Only you can do it, Buffalo-Head. You have to find that ant and give her a helping hand.

TRICKSTER: Me? No.!

SPIDER WOMAN: Yeah, you. You have to fulfull your mission. You have to bring that ant over to the Germ God. She is material for a new world. Then maybe the waterfall will come to earth.

COYOTE: You'd better do it.

TRICKSTER: No. You do it.

COYOTE: I wasn't asked to do it.

SPIDER WOMAN: He's got something else to do.

COYOTE: Oh? What's that?

(The ANT cries out, off.)

SPIDER WOMAN: Buffalo-Head, you go and find that ant!

TRICKSTER: Wait a minute! I have a few more things to say here!

COYOTE: I thought you didn't want to talk anymore.

TRICKSTER: That was before!

SPIDER WOMAN: Say what you have to say and get moving! *(The ANT cries out.)* Hurry!

COYOTE: What do you want to talk about?

TRICKSTER: I forgot.

COYOTE: Come on!

TRICKSTER: Kissing! What is this thing about kissing? Does it spread germs? Do you like kissing? I don't know if I like kissing or not anymore. I'm confused about it. What do you think? *(CLOWN starts throwing dirt at him.)* All right! I remember now! It's a story! There was this false preacher who spread a lot of lies. I want this on the record! He was part of bringing the Fourth World down. But he didn't know it. Or maybe he did, but he wouldn't admit it! He was talking about missionaries, spread all over the world, places where they couldn't fly flags! So, they sat on beds! And they stroked their flags! He was selling sex! And he wouldn't cop to it! He couldn't cop to the fact that he was talking about sex! He was a liar! He brought the Fourth World down!

SPIDER WOMAN: Okay. Thank you very much.

TRICKSTER: He had a lot of money that sonofabitch! He had built a palace made of glass! I saw him on TV last Sunday, that fucking liar! I just wanted this on the record! All right, I'll go and find that ant now, and give her helping hand. *(He wanders upstage, muttering to himself.)*

TWENTIETH EXCHANGE

SPIDER WOMAN: What did you bring me?

COYOTE: Nothing.

SPIDER WOMAN: What did you bring me?

COYOTE: Myself.

SPIDER WOMAN: That's not enough. You must bring me acceptance, as you would the living dead. I gave you life.

COYOTE: I am Coyote!

SPIDER WOMAN: It's you who wants vengeance now. To deny me. To rebuff me.

COYOTE: I'll send you money. Soon as I get a job.

SPIDER WOMAN: I'll take it! I need it! Send money!

COYOTE: I am Coyote!

SPIDER WOMAN: You are nothing. You have nothing, not even money. You're not even intelligent. Muyingwa, the Germ God, has more intelligence than you. Massauwu, the God of the Dead, has more power than you. Even the Owl talks better than you. Even the Beetle walks better than you.

(TRICKSTER, distracted by the fallen "planet" up left, takes a left turn, goes to the planet and stares at it, entranced.)

COYOTE: *(To SPIDER WOMAN)* What do I have to do?

(TRICKSTER, cracking up, pisses on the planet. CLOWN is mortified and the others amazed. TRICKSTER, still laughing, starts back downstage.)

TRICKSTER: Did you see what I did? There were millions of little beings running around on that planet! They were weird—screaming and yelling and carrying on! I pissed on 'em! Ha!

(The ANT screams, off. TRICKSTER, seeing it for the first time, stops. The ANT cries out. TRICKSTER girds himself and goes off toward the sound.)

TWENTY-FIRST EXCHANGE

COYOTE: What do I have to do?

SPIDER WOMAN: *(As the GARGOYLE)* You must come near to me.

COYOTE: I can't come near you. Your odor is offensive to me. Your face is offensive to me. You live in filth. You are the dead alive.

SPIDER WOMAN: Come near to me.

COYOTE: I saw how you knocked on the neighbor's door: "You see! You see, woman! It's my son! My son is here! My son has come to honor me!"

SPIDER WOMAN: What's wrong with that?

COYOTE: I did not come to honor you. How could I honor you?

SPIDER WOMAN: I gave you life. Come and pick me up. Pick me up and carry me. Come on.

COYOTE: I can't!

(CLOWN knocks.)

CLOWN: Pick her up! *(Points to the Germ God)*

SPIDER WOMAN: Come on. Bend a little. Bend your back. Stretch your pain. *(Laughs)* Give it up.

COYOTE: HUUU!

SPIDER WOMAN That's right! A warrior! A warrior has flexibility!

COYOTE: Don't kiss me.

SPIDER WOMAN: I won't kiss you.

COYOTE: Please don't kiss me.

SPIDER WOMAN: I won't kiss you. I'll turn my face away.

COYOTE: *(Struggling)* All right then.

(CLOWN strikes the bell.)

COYOTE: I'll pick you up. I can't stand you, but I'll pick you up. You gave me life.

SPIDER WOMAN: Good, then. Come and carry me. Take me to the Germ God, Muyingwa. I won't kiss you.

COYOTE: I'll come and pick you up. I'll carry you to the Germ God. You gave me life.

(SPIDER WOMAN mounts COYOTE's back, facing away from him. Slowly, COYOTE carries her toward the Germ God. CLOWN, walking backwards, accompanies them, striking the bell softly.)

SPIDER WOMAN: *(As the GARGOYLE)* The insects! I heard them buzzing in the mountains — very strong — talking to me — And then the light went out of me — One breath, that's all it takes, to go down — And then you come up on the other side — sweet — ah ah ah — A man with a bandanna — and no hair— coming to greet me.

CLOWN: The world didn't need anymore height; it already had height. The world didn't need anymore depth; it already had depth. The world didn't need anymore time; it already had time. The world didn't need to be made more complete; it was already complete. The world didn't need to be made more beautiful; it was already beautiful.

(As they enter the Germ God, TRICKSTER appears carrying the wounded ANT on his back. The ANT is man-sized and cries out repeatedly. The Germ God dims up slowly. TRICKSTER and the ANT are the last to enter.)

(The Germ God becomes brightly lit. Music of Tibetan Bells.)

(Blackout.)

END

VII: HE BRINGS THE WATERFALL

SPIDER WOMAN (Christine Avila) recounts the
Insanity of the Two-Leggeds.

Margaret Von Biesen

THE SCENE: Darkness, about an hour before dawn. The Tibetan bell is struck. SPIDER WOMAN and CLOWN, in white costumes, appear in the distance. They approach slowly and majestically, accompanied by tones of the bell. Reaching the outer edge of the playing area — which is a wide area in a canyon, hollow or draw, with the Audience facing a steep rise to the East — SPIDER WOMAN stops suddenly and takes a severe pointing posture. Then she drops it abruptly and rushes forward, shouting at the Audience:

SPIDER WOMAN: Now you're gonna get it! Now you're gonna get it! Trickster is coming for you now! *PENDEJOS!* He's coming for you! You think you got medical problems now? Don't tell me about your filthy medical problems! I know all the diseases possible for two-legged beings! I've had them all! *CABRONES!*

(She takes the SPIDER WOMAN posture. A beat, then she drops it, races to her right, changes directions, and races upstage left. CLOWN, trying to keep up, falls down.)

SPIDER WOMAN: *(To Audience)* I have a boyfriend who will protect me! He has no hair and wears a red bandanna! *(Laughs)* But who will protect you, eh? *HIJOS DE LA CHISPIADA!* Bones on a scaffold! You hear me!? You'll be bones! Less than bones! Bone ash! *(Laughs)* I can't wait!

(Suddenly she shows the five directions, each supported by a drumbeat. Then the steady rhythm of the drum continues as SPIDER WOMAN and CLOWN make a procession down centerstage toward the Audience.)

SPIDER WOMAN: I have seen the new colors in the sky! I have tasted the new flavors in the earth! It was not pleasant to me! It was not aggreeable to me! *(TRICKSTER is heard off, as OWL.)* Wait! Listen!

CLOWN: Trickster is angry!

SPIDER WOMAN: Yes!

CLOWN: Divine is sunlight! Divine is Earthmaker's tent! Divine is the Spider Lady's posture!

SPIDER WOMAN: The fish have cancer! The bones have plague!

CLOWN: Trickster is merciless!

SPIDER WOMAN: Yes! *(COYOTE is heard off, as BLUE JAY.)*

CLOWN: Divine is thunder! Divine is lightening! Divine is Coyote's journey from beginning to end!

SPIDER WOMAN: Yes!

CLOWN: Everyone is pleading for mercy!

SPIDER WOMAN: Yes! We have to kill all the people now! We will use a destroying fire! After that, a big man will come walking over the Earth! He will go around planting new people! *(They stop in front of the Audience.)*

CLOWN: I love Trickster, but he has a magnificent vengence! Everyone will suffer and die! *(Pause)*

SPIDER WOMAN: I had better go among the people now.

CLOWN: *(Amazed)* What for?

SPIDER WOMAN: To protect them from the wrath of Trickster.

CLOWN: But you don't like the people very much!

SPIDER WOMAN: I have to keep my personal feelings out of this. *(She goes to her place just left of the Audience. To CLOWN.)* You take over here.

CLOWN: *(Fearfully alert)* Right!

SPIDER WOMAN: *(To Audience)* Earthmaker said, "I will send messages to the Earth through the spirits of the people who reach me but whose time to die has not yet come. They will carry messages to you from time to time. When their spirits come back into their bodies, they will revive and tell you their experiences."

(COYOTE appears in a distant tree as BLUE JAY. He squawks and flaps his wings.)

SPIDER WOMAN: *(To Audience)* We have gone to the Planet of the Spider People and to Other Side Camp. We have brought the material for a new world into the body of the Germ God, Muyingwa... So you can let that ant go now, Child.

CLOWN: Oh, the ant!

SPIDER WOMAN: Yes. Let her go.

(CLOWN fumbles in a tiny purse and then gingerly, gently, puts the tiny ant on the ground with a finger. TRICKSTER appears in a distant tree as OWL. He hoots and flaps his wings.)

SPIDER WOMAN: *(To Audience)* When the Owl is heard, someone dies. So try not to listen to that Owl. That's Trickster in that Owl. Try not to listen... that's how Owl will steal your power... don't listen...

(CLOWN points. OWL disappears. The tiny ant seems to be crawling up CLOWN's leg. She jumps.)

SPIDER WOMAN: *(Laughing)* That ant is frightened! I don't blame her! *(Laughs)* Anyway, now it's up to Coyote to bring the waterfall to earth. *(Cackling)* While we're waiting, let me tell you another thing about the Chinese! If you happen to be at an intersection, you'd better be really careful when a Chinaman is coming down the road because the Chinese can't tell red from green and they have no side vision at all! *(She cracks up. CLOWN, embarrassed, claps her hands and shushes her. SPIDER WOMAN comes to her senses.)* Trickster will kill any Two-legged he can find, especially the White-eyes. I'll protect you as much as possible, but there's a limit to even what I can do. I'm going to need the help of... Coyote. If Coyote will help me with Trickster's vengeance, then the waterfall will come to earth. *(Sighs)* But you never know with Coyote.

(COYOTE comes running into the space. The drumbeat ceases.)

COYOTE: Hello!

CLOWN: Hello!

COYOTE: My name is Brown.

CLOWN: *(Offering her hand)* How do you do?

COYOTE: *(Sniffing her hand)* I do everything well, thank you.

SPIDER WOMAN: *(To Audience)* That person there is really Coyote.

COYOTE: Have you seen a Buffalo around here?

CLOWN: No, I haven't!

SPIDER WOMAN: *(To Audience)* He doesn't look like much, but he is Coyote all right. *(COYOTE smiles at the Audience.)* He's trying to act charming. Don't fall for it, that's how he steals your power. Just watch him out of the corner of your eye.

(CLOWN turns to keep COYOTE in the corner of her eye. He follows. They make a complete turn.)

COYOTE: You must be the Queen of this planet, otherwise known as Spider Woman?

CLOWN: No, I'm not.

COYOTE: Oh. Have you seen an Owl around here?

CLOWN: Yes, I saw an Owl!

COYOTE: *(Alerted)* Where?

CLOWN: *(Pointing)* There!

(COYOTE Takes his protective posture, then becomes COYOTE. Silently, slowly, he looks intently all around, making a complete turn. Satisfied that OWL is not near, he drops it, starts to go, changes his mind and returns to CLOWN.)

COYOTE: By the way, you look very familiar to me, only different. Are you a relative?

CLOWN: *(Insulted)* No, I'm not!

COYOTE: What's your personal history?

CLOWN: I came into this life a Human Being, with parents. I didn't know if I could do it. I hit the road. I ate many powerful substances and took a lot of abuse from people. But now I'm Clown-Divine.

COYOTE: So what is your place around here?

CLOWN: I am the Chief Clown! I am boss of all the Clowns!

COYOTE: I am First Clown!

CLOWN: I am the Chief Clown! I am boss of all the Clowns!

COYOTE: Show me something then.

CLOWN: *(Pointing)* Mister! Did you see that?

COYOTE: What?

CLOWN: It rained! It rained for the flutter of an eye! Did you catch it?

COYOTE: No.

CLOWN: It was a fantasy!

(A single drumbeat. CLOWN points to a spot in the ground centerstage.)

CLOWN AND SPIDER WOMAN: A deep unease, there, under the gravel! Under the rocks! Disturbed! Unhappy!

(TRICKSTER appears upstage behind some rocks and dead branches. He speaks as COYOTE's father with a mournful wail.)

TRICKSTER: COYOTE!

COYOTE: *(Kneeling)* It's my father, dead in the ground, buried in the arms of Massauwu!

TRICKSTER: I was a bad man, Coyote, a stupid man, a slave to lust, a helpless man! Now all my chances are gone forever, and my bones lie in the darkness of Massauwu!

COYOTE: The nose is gone, the ears are gone, the eyes are gone, the sex organs are gone... His bones lie in the darkness of Massauwu!

TRICKSTER: She has forgiven me, Coyote, she has forgiven me all... that I'd done... but she weeps, Coyote, she weeps day and night...

COYOTE: *(Backing away)* It's a trick!

TRICKSTER: *(Rising)* Ha! It's time now for revenge! Revenge for all the stupidity and the filth! Revenge for the torture! Revenge on the know-it-alls! Revenge on the grabbers! Revenge on the hysterics! Revenge on the fuck-you guys! The smug! Those smegma-heads! The ambitious! The who-gives-a-shits! Revenge on the petulant and the ones with grievances! Revenge on the company guys and the patriots, the big wheels and the profiteers! Revenge on the ordinary! Revenge on the teachers, the knuckle-beaters and baby-fuckers! Revenge on the politicians! Revenge on all the lying sonsofbitches! Revenge! Heh, heh, watch out for the Owl, Coyote, watch out for the Crow!

(TRICKSTER becomes CROW, cawing as COYOTE runs off howling.)

SPIDER WOMAN: *(To Audience)* There he is! Watch out now, watch out!

(TRICKSTER drops the CROW, picks up a large rock, and slowly, menacingly, approaches the downstage playing area and the fearful CLOWN.)

SPIDER WOMAN: *(To Audience)* Remember, that person there is really Trickster. He is pretending to be cool, but he knows you're there. Remember, he wants to steal your power, he wants to kills you! That's how Trickster goes around. Just watch him out of the corner of your eye...

(CLOWN looks at TRICKSTER out of the corner of her eye and he drops the stone he was going to bash her with.)

TRICKSTER: Heh, heh. My name is Smith... Who are you?

CLOWN: I am Chief of all the Clowns.

TRICKSTER: What? You can't be a Chief!

CLOWN: Why not?

TRICKSTER: *(Guffawing)* You're a woman!

CLOWN: I am boss of all the Clowns!

TRICKSTER: *(Laughing)* Okay, show me something.

(CLOWN shows him her breasts. He gazes at them a moment.)

TRICKSTER: No. That doesn't make me feel any better. That's no answer to the problem. That's just stinking flesh. That doesn't get it. *(CLOWN, hurt, turns away.)* Show me something else. *(CLOWN does nothing.)* That's no good, that's nothing. Nothing is nothing. It's not funny. It's not funny at all. *(He finds a very large club.)* I am going to crush you now!

CLOWN: *(Falling to her knees)* Spider Grandmother! Spider Grandmother!

SPIDER WOMAN: *(To Audience)* No one move! Not a muscle! Not an eyelash!

(TRICKSTER fiercely begins circling CLOWN, pounding the earth with his club.)

TRICKSTER: Tell me about these here bones!

CLOWN: Bones!

TRICKSTER: The bones! The bones!

CLOWN: Bones! Especially of a limb! Any part or piece of the hard tissue forming the skeleton of most full-grown vertebrate animals, especially a piece between the two joints! The hard tissue is the skeleton, hence — the body, living or dead!

TRICKSTER: The bones! The bones!

CLOWN: A bone-like substance or thing, a thing made of bone or bone-like material! Flat sticks used as clappers by endmen in minstrel shows for keeping time to music! *(Pause)* The end-man in a minstrel show himself! *(Pause)* Dice! *(Pause)* I feel it in my bones! *(Pause)* I have a bone to pick! *(Pause)*

(Using glowing white sand, TRICKSTER quickly makes a large circle around her.)

CLOWN: Bone ash! A white porous ash prepared by burning bones in the open air, and consisting chiefly of calcium phosphate! Used as fertilizer!

(She is near tears. TRICKSTER picks up his club and prepares to charge her.)

TRICKSTER: Now you will pay for all the sufferings of the Earth!

SPIDER WOMAN: Dig, Child!

(CLOWN frantically digs in the ground, uncovering a large, shining buffalo skull. TRICKSTER is mesmerized by it.)

TRICKSTER: I went down, down. I came to a lake. There on the other side of the lake was the man, standing on a buffalo head, pointing at me. The buffalo head was shining white, white as the salt flat, hot white. The man was pointing at me. I looked up. It was the roof of a cave, sky-blue...

(COYOTE appears way in the distance.)

COYOTE: *(Pointing)* DON'T KILL ME!

(TRICKSTER takes his protective posture. COYOTE vanishes. BOY COYOTE appears off in the bushes, right, as BLUE JAY. TRICKSTER, sensing him, points.)

TRICKSTER: There!

(The young BLUE JAY vanishes. TRICKSTER growls. CLOWN cowers. TRICKSTER eyes the Audience. He stomps. He is enraged. He prepares to charge the Audience. BOY COYOTE rushes into the space.)

BOY COYOTE: Buffalo-Head!

TRICKSTER: *(Spinning around)* What?!

BOY COYOTE: Do you remember how it was, Trickster?

TRICKSTER: *(Amazed)* When?

BOY COYOTE: *(Moving cautiously around him toward the CLOWN.)* When you were young, and the land was young, and the air was sweet, and the water was sweet, and the world was in a bright light, and all things had power? Do you remmber?

(TRICKSTER breaks down and cries. BOY COYOTE scrapes away some of the circle of white sand with his foot, releasing the CLOWN, then takes his protective posture.)

BOY COYOTE: Don't kill me, Trickster.

TRICKSTER: I won't kill you. I can't kill you. *(Pounding the earth with his club)* But I am going to kill all of the Two-leggeds, especially the white-eyes! I am going to kill them all! I am going to kill them with a destroying fire! I am going to evaporate them! My vengeance will be magnificent! *(Pounding the earth, he draws near the Audience.)* Not only will I destroy their flesh, but their memories also! And that of their fathers! And their fathers' fathers!

(BOY COYOTE runs off as TRICKSTER charges the Audience, full tilt. A sharp clang — it's as though he has rammed himself into a steel wall.)

SPIDER WOMAN: *(To Audience)* I've put an invisible shield up over here, to protect you. That's just one example of my power.

TRICKSTER: *(Furiously)* First they put me irons! They put shackles on me! They beat me around the head! They kicked my rib-bones in! They kicked in my solar plexus! They stabbed my liver! They tortured me with needles! They poured acid rain on me! They poisoned me with rays! They broke my heart! And now they've put up a fuckin' shield! Another fuckin' shield! *(He begins to back off, right.)* Well, I'll be back! I'll be back! *(He becomes CROW.)* I've got plans!

(Cawing, he vanishes. COYOTE runs in, left, startling the CLOWN.)

COYOTE: No need to be afraid of me, Clown-Divine! I am Coyote! Coyote is light! He goes about with leaps and bounds!

CLOWN: Bully for Coyote!

COYOTE: I can see that you're not feeling so secure at this time,

because of that other guy around here. Well, not to worry...
(Leaning against the "shield") I can handle him all right. *(BOY TRICKSTER appears in the bushes, left, as CROW. COYOTE points. BOY TRICKSTER disappears. COYOTE smiles at the Audience.)* Today, I realized that the person I was when I was going around and walking and talking with people is the person Coyote is as far as other people are concerned when I am going around.

CLOWN: And?

COYOTE: I always thought I was somebody else going around in whatever body I happened to be in at the time and that that somebody was a secret known only to Coyote.

CLOWN: And?

COYOTE: He is REALLY a great guy, that one! *(CLOWN is appalled. COYOTE smiles, looks up. CLOWN looks up. COYOTE looks at CLOWN.)* Why are trying to turn a quiet moment into a tragedy? *(CLOWN is doubly appalled. COYOTE smiles at the Audience. TRICK-STER appears, up right.)* Here comes something. Ahem. *(Going to TRICKSTER)* In order to be a bona fide warrior, first you have to be a human being. I did that!

TRICKSTER: What's a fuckin' warrior?

COYOTE: A warrior always knows what time it is.

TRICKSTER: I am a hunter, a stalker, and a spy!

COYOTE AND CLOWN: Three things, huh?

TRICKSTER: Right! *(CLOWN whistles.)*

COYOTE: You remember pissing on that planet?

TRICKSTER: Which one?

COYOTE: Which one?! The one you pissed on!

TRICKSTER: Oh, yeah, that one.

COYOTE: Then you got nothing to talk about. A guy who goes around pissing on other people' planets has got nothin' to talk about.

TRICKSTER: It was a tiny planet.

COYOTE: So?

TRICKSTER: So, nothin'! What are you, some kind of good guy? *(Goes behind an upstage bush to take a leak.)*

COYOTE: I am a very nice guy! And I'm handsome, too, and quite talented!

(BOY TRICKSTER appears from behind the bush, buttoning his fly.)

BOY TRICKSTER: You are a flea-bitten, canine bag of bones, and I'm going to cut your balls off and feed them to the crows!

COYOTE: *(Amazed)* Why?

BOY TRICKSTER: *(Throwing gravel at him)* Because you want to steal my women, that's why!

COYOTE: No, I don't! Not all the time! Some women are good for some things, some women are good for other things, and some women—

BOY TRICKSTER: You jerk!

COYOTE: —Are good for nothing. *(BOY TRICKSTER throws more gravel at him.)* Hey, I don't want to fight! I want to eat! I've become a human being!

BOY TRICKSTER: Eat? Eat what? The fish have cancer, the bones have plague.

COYOTE: I think I'll eat you.

BOY TRICKSTER: You don't have the stomach for it.

COYOTE: I love Buffalo meat! Buffalo meat is my favorite food to eat! NUMERO UNO! *(SPIDER WOMAN laughs.)* That woman sure laughs a lot! She also has the habit of asking a lot of questions! That kind of behaviour is rude!

BOY TRICKSTER: Yeah! And she's put a shield up over there! But as soon as that Spider Lady has to take a leak, I'm going to kill all those people she's got with her!

SPIDER WOMAN: Ha! When the Spider Lady takes a leak, the world turns upside down, you little twirp!

BOY TRICKSTER: Did you hear that?

COYOTE: Yeah. But you don't want to kill all those people. If we kill all the people, the white-eyes especially, we'll just be adding to the pile of bodies, the long line of the Dead. What we have to do now is bring the waterfall. *(Makes the spiralling gesture as BOY TRICKSTER becomes OWL.)*

BOY TRICKSTER: I don't see it that way.

COYOTE: You don't?

BOY TRICKSTER: No. Now I think we have to accomplish some vengeance.

COYOTE: Hmmm. Okay. Uh, I heard you went to the center of the Earth.

BOY TRICKSTER: Damn right I did.

COYOTE: How hot is it down there, exactly?

BOY TRICKSTER: Five thousand degrees.

COYOTE: Thank you. *(Becomes HARE and rushes off, right.)*

CLOWN: *(To BOY TRICKSTER)* Hi, Mr. Owl!

BOY TRICKSTER: What was that idiot Rabbit talking about?

(BOY COYOTE enters as HARE. A freeze as OWL and HARE face each other. Then they drop it.)

BOY COYOTE: Dig this: The Center of the Earth, the Core.

BOY TRICKSTER: Yeah?

BOY COYOTE: It's hot. Five thousand degrees.

BOY TRICKSTER: I just told you that!

BOY COYOTE: What is it?

BOY TRICKSTER: It's iron!

BOY COYOTE: Aha!

BOY TRICKSTER: Hey! Fuck off! I'm having a good time here!

BOY COYOTE: Doing what?

BOY TRICKSTER: I'm getting ready to kill all of the Two-leggeds!

BOY COYOTE: And then?

BOY TRICKSTER: Then I'll take a rest in the lap of my Grandmother! Ha!

BOY COYOTE: I think I'll keep on going around, myself. (Looking at the Audience) But you'll never get through that shield. That Spider Lady has got strong legs. I don't know why she does that. She doesn't like them very much, but she still protects them.

BOY TRICKSTER: I don't understand it either. They gave the fish Cancer. They gave plague to the bones of our fathers. Them! The white-eyes! The Two-leggeds! Them! All those ones going around that are not us!

BOY COYOTE: (Pointing to the Buffalo skull) That Buffalo Head Bone is attached to the Long Line of the Dead.

BOY TRICKSTER: So?

BOY COYOTE: I heard that if we played the game of pulling that Buffalo Head around that circle, we would bring peace to the bones of our fathers.

BOY TRICKSTER: Who told you that?

BOY COYOTE: My brother the Bear, my sister the Onyx, my cousin the Zebra, my sister the Lynx —

CLOWN: Clown-Divine!

BOY TRICKSTER: Shut up!

BOY COYOTE: And Clown-Divine. *(BOY TRICKSTER howls indignantly.)* Uh, oh. *(BOY TRICKSTER charges the Audience — a metallic clang as he bounces off the invisible shield.)*

BOY TRICKSTER: Oh, my head! I'm going to kill that Spider Woman! I am going to crush her! I am going to stomp on her! And then these people are finished! *(Starts off)*

BOY COYOTE: Where ya goin'?

BOY TRICKSTER: Watch out! I'll be back! I've got plans! Watch out for the Crow, Coyote! Watch out for the Owl! I've got plans!

(BOY TRICKSTER goes off. SPIDER WOMAN charges into the space, chasing BOY COYOTE away.)

SPIDER WOMAN: Get out of here, you canine runt! Good! Good! Good! *(Gasping)* Come here, Clown-Divine.

CLOWN: Here I am, Spider Grandmother!

SPIDER WOMAN: I want to tell you something. *(Indicates where CLOWN should sit)* One day I woke up to a morning bright with Power. The air was scented with flowers and green grass; sweet water flowed in the streams; the four-leggeds were at peace; the insects were singing quiet songs; the flower beings were happy in the sunlight. Then I saw a two-legged white-eyed woman walking in the field near my cave. This woman had a right hand made of two knives cutting, and she was going around stabbing the flowers with her right hand, killing them. She sang while she was killing them. Then she gathered up the corpses of the flower-beings and took them into her hut and put them into water so she could look at and smell the corpses of the flower-beings. That's when I knew... that's when I knew in my heart... that these Two-legged, white-eyed... creatures... were... INSANE.

(Maddened with anger and grief, she eyes the Audience, then races toward them.)

SPIDER WOMAN: *(To Audience)* Massauwu is coming for you now! That's right! It's time, now! At last! Time to clean up the mess! It's time! *(Stops herself)* But Trickster went off thinking! Ha! Trickster can't think! His head will start to vibrate and he'll come back worse than before! *(Pause)* Good! *(To CLOWN:)* Do you know why I say, "Good!"?

CLOWN: No, why?

SPIDER WOMAN: *(Laughing crazily)* Because I took off the shield, that's why! No more shield!

CLOWN: Oh, no!

(Still laughing, SPIDER WOMAN goes up right for a good view of what might happen next. COYOTE comes running into the space.)

CLOWN: Coyote! Don't let him come back! Don't let him come back!

COYOTE: Oh, sure thing. Not to worry. *(Prepares to approach the Buffalo Skull)*

CLOWN: What are you doing?

COYOTE: I have to bring him back.

CLOWN: Oh, no!

COYOTE: I'm going to sing my death song now, and bring him back. *(He kneels above the buffalo skull.)*

> Divine is sunlight
> Divine is Earthmaker's tent
> Divine is the Spider Lady's posture
> Divine is thunder
> Divine is lightning

Divine is Coyote's Journey
From beginning to end
I became a human being
And walked among the two-leggeds
I saw the new colors in the sky
I tasted the new flavors in the earth
It was not pleasant to me
It was not agreeable to me
I saw the bones of my planet
Whitening in Starlight
On a scaffold in Starlight
Made of a subtle wind
Singing a subtle song
Deep as all the dead together
Deep as all the dead together
At once!

(A single drumbeat. TRICKSTER rushes in to attack COYOTE with a large rock.)

TRICKSTER: Sing it, then! Because now you die! *(He stops above COYOTE ready to smash his head in, but is paralyzed.)* I can't kill you!

COYOTE: *(Standing)* Uh, I guess you heard my excellent singing. I found a good spot for singing on this hill right here!

TRICKSTER: *(Dropping the rock, in extreme frustration)* I can't kill this fuckin' idiot! But I will destroy the Two-leggeds! I will find a way! Vengeance is all I have left! That's all there is!

COYOTE: *(Offhand)* Don't resent yourself, Trickster.

TRICKSTER: *(Incredulous)* What?

COYOTE: The trouble with you — is your background.

TRICKSTER: Background?

COYOTE: You have a background of abuse.

TRICKSTER: WHAT THE FUCK ARE YOU TALKING ABOUT?

COYOTE: All I'm saying is, we can't get through the Spider Lady's shield. That shield is made of powerful stuff.

TRICKSTER: Tell me, Coyote, what's it made of?

COYOTE: Uh, time.

TRICKSTER: Time?

COYOTE: It's another time. We can't get... through it.

TRICKSTER: Time? Time? *(Picks up his club and gets ready to charge, but can't help asking one more question.)* What is this here "abuse"?

COYOTE: Don't distract me, Trickster. Everybody has a background of abuse. My advise to you is to put your vengeance into that Buffalo Head Bone.

TRICKSTER: Why?

COYOTE: *(Very annoyed)* Why? How many times do I have to tell you?!

TRICKSTER: *(Furiously)* As many times as you want to! *(Prepares to attack)*

CLOWN: No, wait!

SPIDER WOMAN: Go ahead! Charge! *(Laughs)* Charge!

CLOWN: *(To SPIDER WOMAN)* You stay out of this!

TRICKSTER: *(To CLOWN)* Now, what?

CLOWN: Now, listen...

(COYOTE has become curious about the "shield," decides to inspect it with his nose — quite close to the Audience.)

CLOWN: Listen, Trickster, that bone I dug up for you is attached to the Long Line of the Dead.

TRICKSTER: I've been told that already. I've thought it over. And I don't want to think about it anymore.

CLOWN: Don't think. Just listen. That line goes back through all time and it all comes together here. Right here. Right here is the center of everything. See?

TRICKSTER: No! What I see is murder, greed, cruelty — and abuse!

SPIDER WOMAN: Right!

TRICKSTER: And I'm not gonna sacrifice my pure rage for the sake of these puny Two-leggeds! Fuck 'em. It's five thousand degrees hot down there! They don't mean shit! So fuck 'em!

SPIDER WOMAN: Fuck 'em!

TRICKSTER: Now they've got no more chances!

SPIDER WOMAN: That's the way they want it!

TRICKSTER: I like it! *(CLOWN spits.)*

CLOWN: I cannot waste my time here one moment longer. *(She joins SPIDER WOMAN as COYOTE returns to the scene.)*

COYOTE: I have an idea: you can take care of all your vengeance at once and then you won't have to expend any more energy in that direction.

TRICKSTER: No! You don't tell me nothin'! *(Clubs COYOTE. Turns to Audience. COYOTE bounces back up.)* You don't give me no fuckin' advice! *(Clubs him again. Turns to Audience. COYOTE springs up.)* A fuckin' good guy all of a sudden! *(Clubs him again, turns to Audience. COYOTE bounces up.)* I'm taking care of the problem! *(Clubs him again, goes for the Audience. COYOTE springs up again.)*

COYOTE: You're right! Let's do it!

TRICKSTER: *(Stopped)* Huh?

COYOTE: I am not a good guy! I am Coyote! Let's GO!

TRICKSTER: Wait a minute.

COYOTE: Yeah?

TRICKSTER: This is MY vengeance!

COYOTE: Fine. I won't take any credit for it.

TRICKSTER: Let's go then!

COYOTE: I was just thinking.

TRICKSTER: *(Stopped)* What were you thinking?

COYOTE: If we do it this time, we'll only have to do it again next time.

TRICKSTER: And?

COYOTE: If we do it my way, we do it for ALL time, once and for all.

TRICKSTER: I WANT IT ALL!

COYOTE: There's just one drawback.

TRICKSTER: What's that?

COYOTE: It takes a big man to accomplish such an important mission.

TRICKSTER: I'm the man! Come on!

COYOTE: *(Looking up)* Oh!

TRICKSTER: What?

COYOTE: Look up, Trickster! *(TRICKSTER looks up)* The Earth has sent out feelers!

TRICKSTER: Yeah!

(All four characters reach to the sky as if touching many strands of light.)

COYOTE: They go all the way up to the stars!

TRICKSTER: Yeah!

COYOTE: She is feeling around up there for help... *(TRICKSTER starts to cry.)* Listen. There's only one thing to do. You have to put all your vengeance into the Buffalo Head Bone. And I'll pull that bone around that circle. And then the waterfall will come to Earth. That's all that's left.

TRICKSTER: *(Going to the Buffalo Skull)* That's all that's left.

COYOTE: That's it.

TRICKSTER: That's it.

COYOTE: *(Taking the Warrior posture)* HUUU! *(TRICKSTER is brought to his knees above the skull. SPIDER WOMAN and CLOWN move further up the hillside.)*

SPIDER WOMAN: We traveled in the Germ God...

CLOWN: Muyingwa!

SPIDER WOMAN: A long way we traveled...

CLOWN: In an instant!

SPIDER WOMAN: With the material...

CLOWN: For a new world!

SPIDER WOMAN: An ecstatic journey we made...

CLOWN: And we saw the bones! *(COYOTE is ready now to pull the buffalo skull around the circle.)*

COYOTE: Let's go.

SPIDER WOMAN: They came to this land, and this is what they said!

COYOTE: *(As he starts to pull)* This is what they said!

TRICKSTER: *(With great force, reflecting tremendous inner conflict)* This land is Paradise. This place is a boon to Mankind. We got freedom here. We can worship whatever we want here. Oh, the water is sweet. Oh, the air is sweet. And there is every kind of food here in abundance. We can have time here. We can worship what we want here. First, we'll clear the vermin off the land. Those ones that are not us, that don't believe as us. Then we'll cut up the land in pieces, and everybody can own a piece of land. And we'll clear the land and plant food in the land, because the game won't last forever. We can worship whatever we want here. We'll buy and sell the land we cut up. We'll buy and sell the food we grow. We'll have cattle ranches and stockyards. And we'll create wealth. We'll get wealth out of the land and out of the ground. And we'll create power. We can worship whatever we want here. And we'll find energy. We'll cut into the land for energy and power. And we'll get energy from the water. And we'll keep the vermin out of the way. Those who don't believe as us, who aren't one of us, who aren't in this thing with us. We'll fence 'em and we'll feed 'em, but we'll keep 'em out of the way, because there's nothing like this wealth, and there's nothing like this power. And we can worship what we want here. And we'll cut our way through the mountains and cross the rivers and valleys, and we'll be moving, we'll be on the move, we're moving, moving, creating wealth, creating power, and it has to be fed, it has to be fed with ENERGY! WE'LL FIND THAT ENERGY! WE WORSHIP WHAT WE WANT TO! WE'LL CUT INTO THE LAND FOR ENERGY! WE'LL DAM THE RIVERS! WE'LL CUT THROUGH BEDROCK! WE'LL CUT THROUGH MATTER! WE'LL FIND MORE! MORE! WE WORSHIP WHAT WE WANT!

(TRICKSTER collapses as COYOTE completes the circle with the buffalo skull.)

SPIDER WOMAN AND CLOWN: LET'S GO!

COYOTE: *(Dragging TRICKSTER)* Come on!

SPIDER WOMAN AND CLOWN: LET'S GO!

COYOTE: Wait a minute! *(TRICKSTER can barely crawl.)*

SPIDER WOMAN: What are you making such a big deal out of it for?!

CLOWN: Big deal!

SPIDER WOMAN: What you did is nothing!

CLOWN: Nothing!

SPIDER WOMAN: Child's play! Nothing!

CLOWN: Child's play! Nothing!

SPIDER WOMAN: Let's go!

COYOTE: Give us a helping hand!

SPIDER WOMAN: No way, fool! You ain't done nothing until you can climb up the side of this hill now! Come on!

CLOWN: Come on!

(COYOTE and TRICKSTER struggle up the hill, regaining their strength.)

ALL TOGETHER: *(As they climb toward the rim)* THIS IS WHAT EARTHMAKER SAYS: COYOTE AND MYSELF, WE WILL NOT BE SEEN AGAIN UNTIL EARTHMOTHER IS OLD AND DYING. THEN WE WILL RETURN TO EARTH, FOR IT WILL NEED A CHANGE BY THAT TIME. COYOTE WILL COME ALONG FIRST, AND WHEN YOU SEE HIM YOU WILL KNOW THAT I AM COMING. WHEN I COME ALONG, ALL THE SPIRITS OF THE DEAD WILL BE WITH ME. THERE WILL BE NO MORE OTHER SIDE CAMP. ALL THE PEOPLE WILL LIVE TOGETHER. EARTHMOTHER WILL GO BACK TO HER FIRST SHAPE AND LIVE AS A MOTHER AMONG HER CHILDREN. THEN THINGS WILL BE MADE RIGHT!

(They form a tableau on the rim of the hill and make a keening sound. A bright light — the sun — appears behind them. The waterfall comes to Earth.)

END

"The Earth has sent out feelers!"

Margaret Von Biesen

NOTES

Figure 1. The hole in the ground and tree that are the set for *I: Pointing.* Some of Coyote's tools are visible on Darrell Larson's back, right.

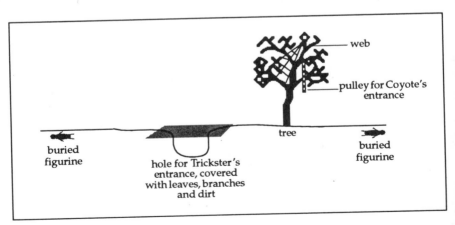

Figure 2. Set diagram for *I: Pointing.*

I: POINTING

Coyote, in Native American story and myth, moves with ease and mishap between the world of Nature and the Spirit World (ultimately One). A transformative creature, he manifests — depending on the time of day, the circumstances, and his digestion — animal, human and divine characteristics. Always hungry and on the lookout, bumbling and prone to idiotic mistakes, he is nevertheless immortal. Because of his sly ways, gamesmanship, cunning, and Sage airs, he is also known as Trickster.

In *The Coyote Cycle*, Coyote/Trickster is Two: Coyote jumps down from the sky above, Trickster erupts upward from the center of the Earth.

* * *

A chief interest of ours from the beginning was how to achieve strong theatricality in outdoor conditions. One method of approach was an exercise derived from Carlos Casteneda (*A Separate Reality*, Simon & Schuster) which we called "Finding the Spot," or "Pointing." An actor enters the space, and through a process of sensing, concentration, and alert oberservation, finds a "spot." It is the right spot, the only spot, and has "meaning." He tries to express this meaning through a process of sound and movement.

This exercise was developed in several ways, but most importantly: the actor's path to, and communication of, the "spot" is traced, or stalked, by his partner, who, in the position of hunter, is watchful for a break in the other's concentration, or for any false or inappropriate move, and when this occurs, he points: "There!" (figure 3).

Pointing became a key to the whole evolution of *The Coyote Cycle* and is one of its most pungent grammatical signs. The image for it comes from a Coyote story, wherein Coyote is mesmerized by what he thinks is a man pointing at him from the other side of a lake (as in the cover image). He stands there for days. Finally, someone comes along to tell him that the "man pointing" is really nothing but a stick in a bush.

* * *

For more on the Coyote stories, see especially *Giving Birth to Thunder Sleeping with his Daughter (Coyote Creates North America)*, by Barry Holstun Lopez, Andrews & McMeel, publishers.

POSTURES

The Point

• Unless otherwise stated (as after Coyote's entrance, when he must be careful to point in the Four Directions) a Point can be in any direction.

• It must be all of a piece and precise–head straight, back straight, legs straight, eyes still; feet, arm, finger, head, eyes, all in the same direction. The left arm is down (NOT like the woodcut on the cover, see figure 3).

• It is taken quickly and all at once, with a quarter turn to the right and the cry: "There!"

• It is dropped quickly and all at once.

• It is done preferably with quiet, as opposed to hysterical, force. The idea is to create energy, not throw it away.

• Note that Spider Woman and Clown's points are slightly different (see notes for *II: The Shadow Ripens*).

The Protective Postures

Coyote and Trickster have "protective postures" they must take when the other Points.

• Coyote: right arm straight up, palm facing out, left arm out, palm down, head up, a cry of "AH!" (plate 1). This is the same as his "Obiesant" posture.

• Trickster: partial squat, right forearm across abdomen, left arm covers face, positions very square, accompanied by a grunt and a fierce demeanor (plate 2).

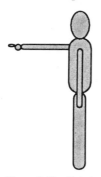

Figure 3. The Point

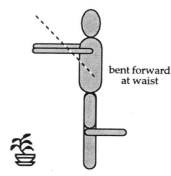

bent forward
at waist

Figure 4. Coyote's plant
listening posture

Coyote's plant listening posture
Bent toward the plant, hands profile, weight on right leg, left leg squared behind him (figure 4).

Trickster's sounds and gestures when unearthing the figurines
Five small straw figurines are buried equidistant from each other on the perimiter of the playing space. As Trickster unearths them, he demonstrates each with a corresponding sound and gesture. The sounds and gestures are done with great force, balanced by extreme economy and precision.

"BECOMING"

Coyote and Trickster are capable of transformation into other beings. Each has a repertoire. Coyote's includes Hare, Blue Jay, Woman Coyote. Trickster's includes Old Man, Owl (plate 3), Crow, Buffalo. These must be practiced, of course, but the trick, as with the pointing, is to be absolutely precise, economical and quick. They must be taken all at once and one hundred per cent, and then dropped the same way. Each has inner and outer characteristics, postures, movements, attitudes and sounds, which, once found by the actor, must then be available immediately, on call. There should be no doubt about these transformations in anyone's mind.

When Coyote becomes "Coyote," this implies a light touch. Just enough, just the essence. The foundation of the "character" of Coyote is in the Pointing exercise described above, the basic work of the Coyote actor, which prepares him for his transformative role-playing, including a precise "Coyote:" head swinging side to side, tongue out, body lower to the ground, etc., manifested at appropriate moments. Thus also the "stalking" Coyote.

SOUND EFFECTS & MUSIC

• An eagle bone whistle is blown by Coyote on his entrance.

• A buffalo horn is trumpeted (off) on Trickster's entrance.

• Ceremonial rattles (off) accompany the "battle."

THE SET

Note that seven diffierent site-specific sets are required in an outdoor area allowing maximum variety of terrain. For example, the space for *VII: He Brings the Waterfall* must be dominated by a rise of ground suitably high enough for the engineering of a proper waterfall, east of the Audience.

The set for *I: Pointing* (figures 1, 2) is a large tree; a deep hole dug for Trickster; a rope net in the tree; a playing area; and surrounding space (three-quarters) for the Audience. Coyote is helped on his fall from above by a pulley apparatus hidden in the tree.

The *Cycle* moves from dusk to dawn, with *Pointing* occuring at twilight and *He Brings the Waterfall* ending at sunrise. The Audience is guided to and from each play from a central waiting area by ushers.

COSTUMES & PROPS

Coyote wears a leather jacket, tee-shirt and sneakers (figure 1). He also wears:

- A silver arrow.
- A bear bladder (can be constructed with inflatable rubber.)
- Several weapons. These are handmade stone axes and such, easily breakable.

Trickster wears a hat, dark suit , vest, and tie. Bones accompany him on his entrance (figure 1 & photo, p. 16). His face is mud-encrusted.

II: THE SHADOW RIPENS

Spider Woman, in Hopi Legend, is Goddess of the Earth. Therefore, she occupies a very important place in the Solar System, including power over gravity, the atmosphere, volcanic forces, etc. Ultimately, she is responsible for the destiny of the spirit of Coyote/Trickster, bound up as this is with the fate of the Earth. In *The Coyote Cycle*, she demonstrates all of these powers in an often frustrated attempt to guide Coyote/Trickster towards the fullfillment of his mission. Along the way, she is also responsible for informing us about the Creation of the Worlds according to the Hopi.

Like Coyote, Spider Woman is a transformative being, manifesting as Goddess and Hag, Earth Mother and Homeless Crazy Woman, Spider Grandmother and Gargoyle. Powerful as she is, she can shift between these aspects of herself without transition, completely, all at once. For more on Spider Woman, see *Spider Woman Stories* by G. M. Mullett, University of Arizona Press, and *Book of the Hopi* by Frank Waters, Penguin.

Clown is a composite, with roots in both the Hopi Koshari or Pueblo Kosa traditions of the Southwest, and American vaudeville. She is a mute Female person who has been taken under Spider Woman's protection as an Apprentice. In *The Shadow Ripens*, she can only hand-sign and grunt.

* * *

For this play, we began with sound and movement exercises working with gravity: the weight of the body, the pull of the Earth. We created "gravity holes," places where the pull was lessened or increased. (Spider Woman puts on the gravity or takes it off, as she wills.)

The Shadow Ripens, on one level, is about "one-heartedness." In spite of Coyote/Trickster's helplessness in the face of Spider Woman's power and his own clumsiness, impulsiveness, and trickiness, he is always given another chance. This time he must turn to his "good deities" (advice from the Hopi creation myth). We interpret one-heartedness to mean a pure sound and movement, of necessity new each performance, simple and direct and pleasing to the "Gods." Spider Woman does have the option (never employed by us) of refusing to take off the gravity. Coyote/Trickster is freed by his one-hearted response, but a moment later he blames the stars. He will go up there and "fix" them. And he reaffirms his belonging also to the Earth: he decides to "get a job as a buffalo."

POSTURES

Spider Woman's posture
Spider Woman takes a characteristic posture whenever she is about to do something important, like fooling with the gravity, bringing the stars down, showing the four directions, etc. (figure 5). Arms horizontally to the sides bent vertically at the elbows, palms facing out, legs widespread in a deep knee-bend, making a foursquare image solidly balanced as in an Oriental martial arts position.

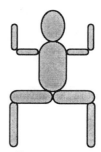

Figure 5. Spider Woman's posture.

Fooling around with gravity

It doesn't take much. Spider Woman performs the task with more or less dramatic flair, supported by special music and the others' reactions (plate 4).

Bringing down the sky

Spider Woman takes a strong position low to the ground with her back straight, and reaches up and gets a good grip on the sky with one hand; she reaches for a grip with the other hand; she slowly brings the sky down as the others duck.

Exchanging the large intestine

Trickster and Coyote face each other close together groaning and carrying on as they mime the difficult transference of this important bodily organ— Trickster pushes as Coyote pulls— then grunt with satisfaction when it is accomplished.

"BECOMING"

Coyote, Trickster, and Spider Woman show many aspects in this play, including Trickster as Old Man, Spider Woman as Coyote's Young Wife, etc. These transformations are not broad, i.e. they are embodied naturally, one hundred percent, subtly, without transitions,

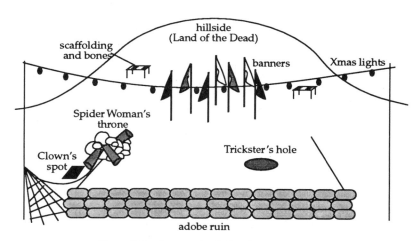

Figure 6. Set diagram for *II: The Shadow Ripens.*

held as long as necessary, and then dropped (see "Becoming" notes for I: Pointing).

When Trickster becomes "Spirit of the Dead," his whole demeanor changes – he stands tall and solemn, becoming quiet, soft-spoken, slow-moving, graceful, dignified: Gravitas. When he approaches the Audience "to say hello to some people," he takes the time to look seriously into people's eyes, to acknowledge them in the present.

SET & PROPS, SOUND EFFECTS & MUSIC

• Coyote wears bells on his ankles.

• Appropriate music for the Land of the Dead sequence (originally composed by Don Preston).

• Play should be performed on the side of a hill, with the ancient adobe floor being the main playing area (figure 6, plate 6).

• Christmas tree lights form a canopy above: The Stars. They make a tinkling sound when they come on.

• Music cue for putting on and taking off gravity.

• A Buffalo head-bone. Male skull of an American Bison, sacred to the Lakota and other Plains Tribes (plate 14).

III: PLANET OF THE SPIDER PEOPLE

SET & PROPS
SOUND EFFECTS & MUSIC

• Set should be in a wooded area if possible (figure 7).

• The rock-costumes should conform to the environment. Trickster and Spider Woman are INSIDE the rocks, which have concealed apertures for seeing, hearing and breathing, and can be miked. They must be easily "shed."

• The Spider People are lots of hairy spiders of all sizes, rigged to be able to move and scurry about on cue (see photo, p. 43).

• Webs.

• The Birthing Hole: When Coyote gives birth on the side of the hill, he takes his position, facing the Audience, right above where there is a camouflaged hole (figure 7). Just under the surface of the ground cover — above the hole — is a real door with a shiny brass doorknob. Trickster "makes" it simply by revealing it. The door opens to reveal the hole, big enough for Clown to crawl half-way inside. Also in the hole are Coyote's 12 spider babies. These are dolls with big faces which look like their names. In midwifing them, Clown attaches each to invisible lines — fishing line — manipulated offstage, and sends them flying, so that when all's done there are 12 spider babies swinging and bobbing above the Audience.

• The Huge Doll is a ten-foot facsimile of the figurines used in *I: Pointing*. It is hidden during the play, and then rises up with the help of manipulators offstage. It must be in exactly the right spot (figure 7) and have glowing eyes.

• Spider Woman's voice is miked and projected through surrounding speakers.

• Strobe lights and static electricity sounds help convey the "shocks."

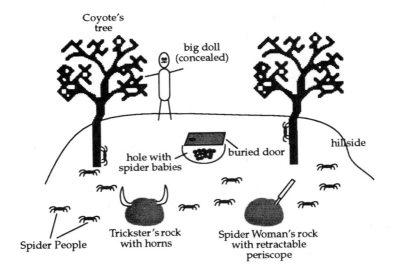

Figure 7. Set diagram for *Planet of the Spider People.*

IV: OTHER SIDE CAMP

"Other Side Camp" is a Native American phrase for the "The World on the Other Side," a Shadow World, an indeterminate Netherworld, a world of the Lost.

We called the exercise for this play "The Two-Legged Walk." A team of actors face each other upstage right and upstage left and prepare to approach one another. They have agreed to find the contact of their feet on the ground and to maintain awareness of that contact for the length of the walk.

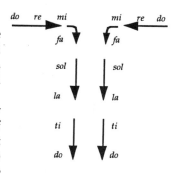

Figure 8. The form of the "Two-Legged" walk.

Eyes are "soft:" it is the body which walks (see photo, p. 54). If sound and movement is employed, the approach is signaled by an initial expression coming up through the feet — not down from the head — and is developed organically as the walk continues. As the actors cross towards each other center stage, an energy is created which will indicate the moment of turning. This is a simple downstage turn, but must be at the right moment, the actors sensing it together. Timing is all. And there is an aesthetic criterion: was the turn beautiful?, was it "right"? Then, side by side, the actors make a downstage processional approach to the Audience. A key moment here is the moment of leaving the exercise. We found it useful to consider the form of the exercise as a musical octave, with the *do* being the moment of beginning, *re* and *mi* the approach, *fa* out of the turn, and *sol, la, ti* the downstage walk, with the *do* of a new octave sounded in front of the Audience. At first, the point is to leave it there, with the potential octave unexpressed — this creates "power."

After much repetition and practice, additional octaves can be added, and the basic form of the exercise elaborated and complicated in several ways, including experiments with posture, the use of impromptu language, texts, and so on; but the form of the walk is the design of the play (figure 8). For more on the octave, see *In Search of the Miraculous*, by P.D. Ouspensky, Harcourt Brace Jovanovich.

POSTURES

• When Spider Woman "shows the Four Directions," she does so out of her Spider Woman posture (see Posture notes for *II: The Shadow Ripens*). She half-turn pivots toward each direction from her posture and Points with alternate arms, keeping her other arm in place. These are done sharply but without rushing and each Point is accompanied by a powerful beat of the drum.

• Spider Woman points to the lights in the ground, again along with the drum. The lights are equidistant from each other and, of course, buried (figure 9).

SET & PROPS

• The set is diagrammed below. See also the photo on page 76.

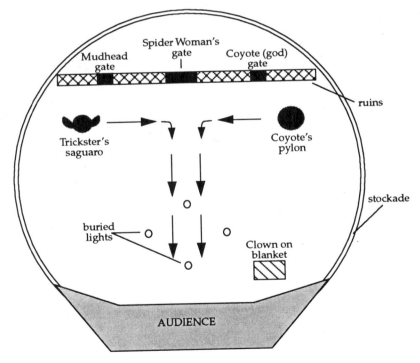

Figure 9. Set diagram for *Other Side Camp.*

• A crew person must translate for Clown at the top of the play.

• Trickster's "skin" is a prosthetic fastened to his back and ripped off by Coyote.

• The masks are: A mudhead mask (plate 2), common in the Southwest, a contemporary Coyote mask, and a Headdress for Spider Woman (plate 9). When worn, they bestow Godlike bearing and grace.

SOUND EFFECTS & MUSIC

• Music during the attempted sex is played by Clown on a toy xylophone keeping time with the offstage drum.

• The best drum was a large one from Taos Pueblo (see back cover photo).

• A harsh note from a whistle accompanies the "skinning" of Trickster.

V: LISTENING TO OLD NANA

The exercise of "Listening with the Whole Body" is at the core of this play and is derived from the Native American understanding of the Intelligence of the Body and the development of the Whole Person, an understanding which is also prominent in many other so-called "primitive" cultures. We were much influenced in this approach, as well as in our general attitudes, by the work of G. I. Gurdjieff. For more on the Apache, see *Apaches*, by James L. Haley, Doubleday.

POSTURES

Listening with the Whole Body

For maximum efficacy, the series of postures signifying "Listening with the Whole Body" are taken under the extreme pressure of an outside command (as from Old Nana), which is unpredictable. The postures must be taken immediately and with one hundred percent precision and then held until the command to change it. The models for some of them were various Kachina dolls (plates 10, 11).

The Warrior posture

A step with the right foot to spread the legs; at the same time knees bent and back straight so that upper body "sits," along with fierce "tying of the knot" gesture at lower abdomen and the cry of "Huuu!"

The "Singing of Insects" posture

Right hand shielding forehead, slow bend backward from the waist, while Trickster does a high-pitched keen and Coyote hisses a "Zzzz" sound. They do this once to complete the series of "Listening" postures, and follow with the Warrior posture. A moment later they do the "Insects" posture five times, each time concluding with a Point in each direction.

Acknowledging the five directions

These are Points, with Coyote starting North and Trickster starting West, the fifth direction being Up.

SOUND EFFECTS & MUSIC

• "The masks speak" is the result of a taped sound cue with speakers in the Mudhead and Coyote masks mounted on the set (plate 9).

• The whistling, the stagecoach, the footsteps, Coyote/Trickster from *IV*, etc., are all taped sound effects also, but Spider Woman is live and miked.

• The Voice of Old Nana is live and miked (one mike for both in the back of the house). He was played by the Author.

SET & PROPS

• The Audience part of the house is covered and enclosed, while the set is open to the sky (plates 2, 9, 10). During all-night performances, this play takes place at about 3 o'clock AM.

• Old Nana's appearance is accomplished by projecting his photograph (see photo, p. 76) onto the "screen" created by waving the white memory stick up and down very rapidly at the focus point of the projected slide.

VI: THE SACRED DUMP

The story of the Four Worlds is related by the Hopi Creation Myth and was first told by the *Cycle* in *Coyote II: The Shadow Ripens*. This is the Fourth World.

The Germ God, MUYINGWA, is the Hopi God of regeneration

and rebirth. In the play he forms a sort of enclosure constructed of branches, brush, bones, etc., which is at the same time visually representative of this Deity (see figure 10, photos p. 98). MASSAUWU is the God of the Dead.

The main exercise for *The Sacred Dump* was a version of the "Two-Legged Walk," extending its length in space and elaborating its complexity of intention, in this way establishing an essential pattern of movement up and down stage with the corresponding rhythms of speech.

POSTURES

Clown's posture of supplication
Head up, arms up and bent at right angles at the elbows, palms facing the sky, right foot forward, back straight. Concluding *V* she does the same (with the added expression of Terror).

Clown gets behind Coyote and Trickster and "pushes them" with her instrument
This is one of the instruments she loans to kids in the Audience, made of rubber band and wood, attached to a length of rope (plate 12). When swung in the air, it makes a winding, roaring sound.

Spider woman's power
As evidence of Spider Woman's great powers, with a mere hand gesture she is able to turn Coyote and Trickster and to pull them by their bellies.

CHARACTERS AND "BECOMING"

• At this point, the Clown is beginning to recover her powers of speech and, under Spider Woman's tutelege, has firmly found her place in the ritual ceremony of the *Cycle*. At first, her attempts to speak are halting and difficult, but by the end of the play she has fully recovered and speaks fluently. As further evidence of her increase in mastery and powers bestowed on her by Spider Woman, Clown carries two "magical" instruments with which she controls the beats of the play: a wooden block, which she knocks, and a Tibetan bell.

• Both "Coyote's Father" and the "Gargoyle" should be taken as complete characters in their own right. One hundred percent, in sharp contrast (see photo, p. 98).

SET & PROPS, SOUNDS & MUSIC

• See figures 10 and 11 for a diagram and photo of the set. See also the photos on page 98.

• The Ant is man-sized, fully operational and naturalistically detailed and true. It's parts (legs and head, etc.) can move, and its eyes shine (plate 13). For its cries, we used hand fog-horn instruments.

• The pre-set music is a taped loop of the "Singing of Insects."

• The musical instruments already mentioned for Clown: a wooden block, a Tibetan Bell, several swinging instruments for Clown and the Audience kids.

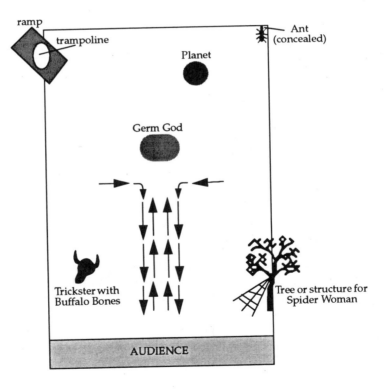

Figure 10. Set diagram for *The Sacred Dump.*

Figure 11. The set for *VI: The Sacred Dump,* showing the Germ God (left) and the Planet (right).

VII: HE BRINGS THE WATERFALL

POSTURES & CHARACTERS

• Boy Coyote and Boy Trickster are real boys, costumed exactly like Coyote and Trickster.

• The "Earth sends out feelers" movement is best described in the photo on page 147 of the text.

• The pulling of the Buffalo Skull (plate 14) is a sacred ceremony in the tradition of the Sundance. In this case, Coyote is not pierced, of course — the Buffalo Skull is attached with straps and ropes to his forehead — but both he and Trickster suffer an ordeal here that cannot be faked.

SET, PROPS & COSTUMES

• The play is timed to end with the crack of dawn.

• The set must be dominated by a rise of ground suitably high enough for the engineering of a proper waterfall, east of the Audience (figure 12). The waterfall is a real waterfall (plate 15).

• For complete surprise in certain of the appearances and disappearances, a trench may have to be dug.

• The Drum is the same one used thoughout the *Cycle* (see photo on inside cover). It is played off stage, but can be visible to the Audience.

• See the photo on page 124 as a good example of Spider Woman's costume.

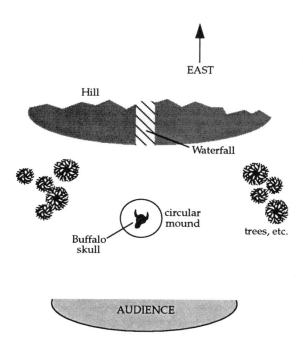

Figure 12. Set diagram for *He Brings the Waterfall.*

Plate 1. COYOTE (Norm Skaggs) takes his protective posture while CLOWN (Rabin Karfo) and SPIDER WOMAN (h. Teirrah McNair) look on in *I: Pointing.*

Plate 2. TRICKSTER (Norbert Weisser) takes his protective posture in the set and costume for *V: Listening to Old Nana.*

Plate 3. TRICKSTER (Norbert Weisser) "becomes" The Owl.

"The Shadow Ripens" Daniel O. Stolpe © 1984 21"x28" Edition 35   Second of a Suite of Seven Images

Plate 4. SPIDER WOMAN (h. Tierrah McNair), center, "fools around with gravity" in *II: The Shadow Ripens*, affecting CLOWN (Robin Karfo), left, and COYOTE (Norm Skaggs).

Plate 5. "I heard overwhelming sounds, like earthquake, like thunder!" TRICKSTER (Robert Behling), foreground, and COYOTE (Norm Skaggs) in *II: The Shadow Ripens.*

Plate 6. Left to right: TRICKSTER (Norbert Weisser), SPIDER WOMAN (Christine Avila), and CLOWN (Priscilla Cohen) in the downstage playing area of *II: The Shadow Ripens.*

"Planet of the Spider People" Daniel O. Stolpe © 1984 21"x28" Edition 35   Third of a Suite of Seven Images

"Other Side Camp" Daniel O. Stolpe © 1984 21"x28" Edition 35   Fourth of a Suite of Seven Images

Chris Singleton Mednick

Plate 7. SPIDER WOMAN (h. Teirrah McNair) "becomes" Homeless Crazy Woman while COYOTE (Norm Skaggs), left, and TRICKSTER (Robert Behling) look on in *IV: Other Side Camp.*

Susanna Styron

Plate 8. "My death song is: SHUT YOUR STARS." COYOTE (Darrell Larson) prepares to "skin" TRICKSTER (Norbert Weisser) in *IV: Other Side Camp.*

"Listening to Old Nana" Daniel O. Stolpe © 1984 21"x28" Edition 35   Fifth of a Suite of Seven Images

Plate 9. The set of *V: Listening to Old Nana* at night, showing the ceremonial deity masks.

Margaret Von Biesen

Plate 10. Left to right: CLOWN (Priscilla Cohen), COYOTE (Darrell Larson) and TRICKSTER (Norbert Weisser) perform the "left knee" listening posture on the set of *V: Listening to Old Nana.*

"The Sacred Dump" Daniel O. Stolpe © 1984 21"x28" Edition 35   Sixth of a Suite of Seven Images

Plate 11. Left to right: COYOTE (Jason Smith), TRICKSTER (Roger G. Smith) and CLOWN (Page Leong) perform the "right knee" listening posture in *VI: The Sacred Dump.*

Plate 12. CLOWN (Page Leong) "pushes" COYOTE (Jason Smith), left, and TRICKSTER (Roger G. Smith) ahead of her with her instrument in *VI: The Sacred Dump.*

Plate 13. TRICKSTER (Norbert Weisser) with The Ant from *VI: The Sacred Dump.*

"He Brings the Waterfall" Daniel O. Stolpe © 1984 21"x28" Edition 35   Last of a Suite of Seven Images

Chris Singleton Medtrick

Plate 15. CLOWN (Robin Karfo) unearths the Buffalo headbone in *VII: He Brings the Waterfall*.

Chas Rundberg

Plate 16. He Brings the Waterfall.

ACKNOWLEDGEMENTS

From the beginning, when we discovered the Pointing exercise together, this work was a joyous collaborative effort between the author and Darrell Larson (Coyote), and Norbert Weisser (Trickster). Rarely does a theatre artist have the opportunity for such a sustained and fullfilling partnership as the three of us had. During those first exploratory years, we were joined at different times by Lorinne Vozoff and Ellen Blake, as Spider Woman, and I must thank them for their invaluable contributions here. In '81, Christine Avila began her ongoing mastery of Spider Woman with *Other Side Camp*, and in that year Priscilla Cohen helped to begin the evolution of Clown.

Matthew Goulish was our longtime stage manager, designer, electrician, traveling companion—and, when exigency demanded it, a superb Coyote; Peggy Dobreer coordinated with devotion for many years; James Parks created the set for *Listening to Old Nana*; Bob Behling became our master set-builder, doll-maker, archivist — and a wonderfully salty Trickster; Don Preston designed lots of our music and sound effects; Karen Musser did all of our first lighting designs; Kim Simons created the original "Spider People;" Kathleen Cramer and Stephanie Curley collaborated on the costumes; Rick Foster of *West Coast Plays* published the plays as they came along and encouraged interviews and articles; Jesse Shepard and Morgan Weisser created, respectively, the original Boy Coyote and Boy Trickster; Sarah Lovett and Alice Sealey facilitated our several expeditions to Santa Fe, culminating in the first complete all-night performance; Dan Stolpe created the seven fabulous wood-cuts, one of which became our poster; Susanna Styron shot a priceless video and photographic record of the all-night production in Santa Fe; Chas Rundberg was instrumental in the engineering and construction of three waterfalls; Susan Loewenberg and Sara Maultsby were responsible for both the L.A. production and the tour to Yugoslavia (Richard Bloom expertly and stalwartly stage managed these); a grateful bow to Cheryl Slean, Padua Hills' publisher, who made this book possible; a special thanks to Richard Williams, our spiritual mentor, guide, and sweat leader; special thanks also to Penny Williams, Selo Black Crow, Leonard Crow Dog and all the men and women of the Red Road, without whose encouragement and support this project would no doubt have gone unfinished or awry.

PRODUCTION HISTORY

The Coyote Cycle was developed serially at the Padua Hills Playwrights' Festival starting with *Pointing* in 1978. All of the first six plays of the series were performed originally at the Padua Hills site in Claremont, California; the seventh, *He Brings the Waterfall*, was premiered at the '84 Festival's venue at the California Institute of the Arts in Valencia, California. Subsequent productions of two or more of the plays were given at the Intersection Theatre of San Francisco; at the Bay Area Playwrights' Festival in Mill Valley; and at the Armory for the Arts in Santa Fe, New Mexico.

The *Cycle* was first presented in its entirety, twilight to dawn, by Theatre-in-the-Red at the Randall Davey Audobon Estate in Santa Fe, New Mexico, on September 30, 1984, with the following cast:

Coyote	Darrell Larson
Trickster	Norbert Weisser
Spider Woman	Christine Avila
Clown	Priscilla Cohen
and	
Boy Coyote	Dakota Fitzner
Boy Trickster	Morgan Weisser

Directed by Murray Mednick

PRODUCTION

Producers	Sarah Lovett & Alice Sealey
Associate Producer	Peggy Dobreer
Set Design and Construction	Robert Behling
Production Stage Manager	Matthew Goulish
Assistant Stage Manager	Kelly Stuart
Chief Scout	Frederick Lopez
Technical Assistant	Chas Rundberg
Lighting Operator	Deborah Scharaga
Assistant Producer	Zoe Viles
House Manager	Rhona Gold
Publicity and Tech.	John Oldach
Lighting Consultant	Dick Hogle

DESIGN

Poster & Coyote Logos	Daniel O. Stolpe
Sound	Don Preston
Costume, Spider Woman II	Dona Granata
Costume, Spider Woman VI	Michele Jo Blanche
Costume, Spider Woman VII	Louise Hayter
Weaving	Nargis
Program Design	Michael Motley
Typography	Casa Sin Nombre, Ltd.
Rocks and Trickster Headdress	Anthony Showe

In the summer of 1985 (July 19 - August 3), *The Coyote Cycle* was presented by L.A. Theatre Works for a one-month run, including two all-night performances (July 27 and August 3), at the Paramount Ranch in Agoura, California, with the following cast:

Coyote	Darrell Larson
Trickster	Norbert Weisser
Spider Woman	Christine Avila
Clown	Priscilla Cohen

and

Boy Coyote	Tavish Graham
Boy Trickster	MorganWeisser

Directed by Murray Mednick

On July 27, Darrell Larson broke his heel at his entrance but courageously finished the all-night performance. Matthew Goulish took over the role of Coyote for the remainder of the run.

PRODUCTION

Producers	Susan Albert Loewenberg
	& Sara Maultsby
Set Design & Constructions	Robert Behling
Production Stage Manager	Matthew Goulish
Structural Engineer	Steve Bauer
Electrician	John Oldach

PRODUCTION (con't)

Hydro-Electric	Chas Rundberg
Production Coordinator	Richard Bloom
Costume Coordinator	Louise Hayter
Photography	Margaret von Biesen
Publicist	Julio Martinez
Box Office Manager	Greg Moreno
House Manager	Eric Schusterman

DESIGN

Sound Design	Gregory Hormel
Costume Spider Woman VII	Louise Hayter
Costume Spider Woman VI	Michele Jo Blanche
Weaving	Margaret Clarke; Nargis
Posters & Coyote Logos	Daniel O. Stolpe
Program	Randi Ganulin
Music	Don Preston

In 1987, *The Coyote Cycle* was presented by American Inroads and The Magic Theater of San Francisco as part of The San Francisco New Performance Festival, in association with L.A. Theatre Works. The play was performed July 9 - August 1, including four all-night performances, at East Fort Baker, Sausalito, in the Golden Gate National Park, with the following cast:

Coyote	Norm Skaggs
Trickster	Robert Behling
Spider Woman	h. Teirrah McNair
Clown	Robin Karfo
and	
Boy Coyote	Andrew Ohren
Boy Trickster	Michael Moir

Directed by Norbert Weisser & Murray Mednick

PRODUCTION

Producer	John Lion, Magic Theater
Scenic Designer	Chas Rundberg
Lighting Design	David Welle
Costume Designer	Gael Russell
Associate Costume Designer	Esther Fishman
Music Design	Don Preston
Sound Consultant	Scott Koue
Stage Manager	Carolyn Campbell
Production Manager	Ann Fujilan
Technical Director	T. Bird
Native American Liason	Richard Williams
Site Manager	Ellen Osborne
Light Board	Eric Graves
Sound Board	John Barnes

In 1988 the *Coyote* Company was invited (through L.A. Theatre Works) to participate in the YUFEST tour of Yugoslavia, along with groups from Mexico, Germany, and Russia. We were able to bring only one of the plays, *The Sacred Dump*, with the addition of a segment from *Listening to Old Nana*. We toured nine cities of what was the then unified nation of Yugoslavia: Belgrade, Skopje, Mostar, Sarajevo, Kotor, Subotica, Novi Sad, Lubijana and Zagreb, performing outdoors in the most astonishing sites — atop ancient city walls, in parks, courtyards, on rooftops, movie studio lots, alleys, along the Danube, on athletic fields — with the following undaunted cast:

Coyote	Jason Smith
Trickster	Roger G. Smith
Spider Woman	Christine Avila
Clown	Page Leong

Produced by L.A. Theatre Works
Directed by Norbert Weisser & Murray Mednick
Stage Managed by Richard Bloom

Pointing, The Sacred Dump, and *Other Side Camp* were performed, respectively, as part of the '89, '90 and '91 Padua Hills' Retrospective Benefits, with the following cast:

Coyote	Darrell Larson
Trickster	Norbert Weisser
Spider Woman	Christine Avila
Clown	Page Leong

Directed by Murray Mednick
Assisted by Cedering Fox

* * *

BIOGRAPHIES

MURRAY MEDNICK was born in Brooklyn, New York. He was for many years a playwright-in-residence at New York's Theatre Genesis, which presented all of his early work (*The Hawk, The Deer Kill, The Hunter, Sand, Are You Lookin'?,* and others). He was Artistic Co-director from '70 to '74, when he emigrated to California. He founded the Padua Hills Playwrights' Workshop/Festival in 1978 and remains its Artistic Director. Plays since then include *The Coyote Cycle, Taxes, Scar, Heads, Shatter 'n Wade, See You in Nairobi* and *Fedunn.* He has been the recipient of two Rockefeller Foundation grants, a Guggenheim Fellowship, an OBIE, and several *Drama-logue* and Bay Area Critics Circle Awards. He edited *Plays from Padua Hills* (1982), and *Best of the West* (1991). His play *Scar,* starring Ed Harris, recently received a critically acclaimed and sold-out run at the MET Theatre in Los Angeles. Other recent productions include a revival of *Heads* at the Omaha Magic Theatre, *Taxes* at L.A.'s New One-Act Theatre Ensemble, and *Shatter 'n Wade* at the Matrix Theatre in L.A. His play *Fedunn* has been given staged readings at the MET Theatre (produced by Ed Harris) and the Odyssey Theatre (produced by Audrey Skirball-Kenis Theatre), L.A. Mr. Mednick was honored with a 1992 Ovation award from the Theatre League Alliance of Los Angeles for his outstanding contribution to Los Angeles Theatre.

DANIEL O. STOLPE (Master Printmaker) works in a tradition of European figurative style, heavily influenced by German Expressionism, to create contemporary interpretations of ancient beliefs. He is represented in over 25 major collections, including Fogg Art Museum, Grunwald Collection (UCLA), the Smithsonian Institution, and the Portland Art Museum. He has received over 50 solo exhibitions nationally and has been the subject of two television documentaries. The genesis of the seven woodcuts in *The Coyote Cycle* evolved out of playwright Mednick's recognition of Stolpe's artistic dedication to the Coyote images in his earlier work, titled "Coyote Suites I & II." After he created "Coyote Pointing," corresponding to the first of the seven plays within the *Cycle*, Stolpe became inspired to create a distinct visual image for each of the seven plays. The seven woodcuts have been published as a limited edition oversized folio with exerpts from each of the plays from the *Cycle*. This monumental work of art has been included in numerous collections nationally, and is also a part of the permanent collection of the Humanities Research Center at the University of Texas at Austin.

CHERYL SLEAN (Publisher) has previously published and co-edited *Best of the West, An Anthology of Plays from the 1990 and 1991 Padua Hills Playwrights Festivals* for Padua Hills Press, and co-edited and designed *Artlines*, for the National Network for Artist Placement. She has been Managing Director of the Padua Hills Playwrights' Workshop / Festival since 1991, when she produced the last Festival of New Plays. A playwright and Padua Hills Workshop alumnus, Slean is a long-time member of the New One-Act Theatre Ensemble (NOTE) in Hollywood, which has produced several of her plays, including *Palmdale, ...And the Leaves of the Trees*, and *Swap Nite*, which received a 1992 *L.A. Weekly* award for Best One-Act Playwriting.

"Mednick's *Coyote Cycle* is a major work of American theatre, born of the land and its people - a warning and a prayer for salvation.

...The natural environment was essential to the work. The settings, derived from Indian designs and religious artifacts, blended with the rigged landscape...

Mednick's theme was continually reiterated -- 'The harsh punishment is coming,' warned the gods, and it is up to mankind to carry out Earth Mother's plans. There were frequent allusions to nuclear holocaust. But the *Cycle* ended on a note of hope, as Coyote's mission was fulfilled. This fusion of art and nature was magical. The audience was clearly uplifted. A sense of renewal prevailed."

A. Richard Sogliuzzo
National Public Radio

"...Beginning at twilight, the audience has been guided from set to set through an atavistic series of worlds where nothing is quite what it appears to be. In *Planet of the Spider People*, rocks speak and spider babies fly out to greet us; in *Listening to Old Nana*, we enter a lean-to kiva with a primitive radar station where bleached bones and adobe bricks make connections with the spirit world. Inside such mysterious environs, the actors make frequently startling appearances. Coyote leaps from trees like a comet hurtling from the heavens, while his cohort Trickster literally digs his way up from the bowels of the earth.

Mixing metaphors like a mad metaphysician, Mednick throws everything into the pot: legends and Lucky Strikes, Milky Ways and mudheads, bag ladies, buffalos, subways and shamans. Out of this potent brew, which uses the Coyote/Trickster traditions and Hopi creation myths as a soup stock, there emerges an intergalactic vaudeville in which the predicaments of the modern age are given new meaning through the mirror of a culture much older and wiser than ours..."

Cree McCree
American Theatre

"What Mednick is after is nothing less than an ecological view of existence. It Infuses everything, from the constant web-image to the physical process of actor and audience involvement... links are made between the Gaelic *Mabinogion*, the Native American myths and the Icelandic sagas. The work is rife with Westernisms as well. But Mednick takes us so far West that we're in the East, carried across a conceptual Bering Strait into the land of Zen where 'arrows go clear through you.' All this exemplifies *Coyote's* great contribution to the contemporary theater: Mednick has created a new kind of anthropologic time capsule."

Robert Koehler
Los Angeles Times

This book was made possible in part by a grant from the City of Los Angeles, Cultural Affairs Department.

Book design, layout & graphics:	Cheryl Slean
Woodcut artwork:	Daniel O. Stolpe
Typesetting:	Jennifer Maisel
Scanning & color separations:	Icon West

Special thanks to Rhythm & Hues, Michael Hacker, Icon West, Rouella Louie of Cultural Affairs, Darrell Larson and Norbert Weisser.

Also available from Padua Hills Press:

Best of the West,
An Anthology of Plays from the 1990 and 1991
Padua Hills Playwrights' Festivals.